POWER BI

A Comprehensive Beginner's Guide to
Learn the Basics of Power BI from A-Z

TABLE OF CONTENTS

Introduction

Microsoft garnered a lot of attention announced its intention to incorporate Self-Service Business Intelligence (BI) in 2009. With that in mind, they released the Power Pivot add-in for Excel in 2010. When Power Pivot was released, it did not come with a massive marketing campaign plan, few announcements and conferences were planned. Due to this, the general awareness of Excel users about this new add-in was poor. And the majority of the users that knew about the new technology were reluctant to adopt it. Professionals in the BI community were not pleased with the response, as there were clear advantages of using the add-in to gather insights from data.

The professionals did not hold back in their response to Microsoft's marketing strategy and pestered Microsoft to expand their promotion of Self-Service BI, and make it appeal to data analysts, decision-makers, data scientists, and BI fanatics all over the world. They also requested an additional feature that allowed them to share reports between a team. Microsoft answered their request by adding a feature called *SharePoint* to the first version of Power BI, SharePoint allows users to share reports offline and online. This still wasn't satisfactory to the professionals who complained about the different bug issues of the version.

Microsoft browsed through all the constructive feedbacks and created the version of Power BI that is currently available. The version was released with a massive marketing strategy, and it applied all the necessary changes and improvements requested by users. As established above, users did not want to use SharePoint to share documents; hence Microsoft excluded it from the features that accompanied the latest version. The users also wanted more power, creative visualizations, mobile experience, and simplicity, which Microsoft delivered in the new version.

A lot of thought, effort, and consideration went into the creation of Power BI. When the users were done observing the updated features, they referred to Power BI as the end-product of the evolution of previous Excel add-ins: Power View, Power Pivot, and Power Query. Power BI can work outside the confines of Excel (the latest version is not dependent on the Microsoft Office installed on your computer).

As of 2019, Microsoft's Power BI is the leading analytics and business intelligence platform available on mobile applications, clouds, on-premise data gateway, data modeling applications, report authorizing applications, and other utilities.

This book offers a comprehensive analysis of the powerful tools and features contained in Power BI's arsenal. It includes the stepwise directions on how to start a Power BI project and how to share the project with a large number of users. As a reader, the book will get you familiarized with the basic concepts of Power BI and how its datasets, dashboards, and reports can be used to give insights and interactive experiences.

This book will help you become conversant with management techniques and administration topics available on Power BI. With the knowledge acquired in the book, you will be able to utilize Power BI's powerful features and carry out successful Power BI projects for your organization.

Who is this Book meant For?

This book targets beginners who are planning to start a career as a business intelligence professional. It is highly recommended for beginners that are totally new to the BI world and are interested in reading introductory data modeling topics on Power BI.

It is also an enlightening read for BI (Business Intelligence) professionals with the responsibility of developing Power BI solutions or handling the management and administration of Power BI projects in their organization.

The book can also serve as a reference resource for BI developers and managers, to aid them in the creation and delivery of successful Power BI projects.

What is Covered in the Book?

Introduction to Power BI – This part is mainly for beginners. It shows how to get started with Power BI, upload data, use quick insights, make reports, decorate reports, create visual interactions, save reports, and manage pages.

Dashboard features – provides guidance on how to invite users from within and outside an organization to see a dashboard, shows how to create a group workspace, and view Power BI reports on mobile devices.

Loading Data from different sources into Power BI desktop – shows readers how to load data into Power BI from different sources of data, explains what Query Editor is, how to load data into Query Editor, and types of data sources. This chapter also gradually guides the reader on how to explore the Power BI desktop.

Data Transformation – shows readers how to transform data with the help of Query Editor. The chapter describes the Query Editor environment, explains the function of each button in the window, and shows how to use them to achieve your goal. The chapter

3

dabbles a bit into the transformation steps possible on Power BI and gives instructions on some of the most popular transformation steps. Steps like how to add, remove, rename, reorder, choose, and filter columns. It also shows how to perform some activities on rows.

Data Models – this bulky chapter goes into the rudimentary of data modeling on Power BI Desktop. It shows you how to create a data model, describes the Power BI Data View environment, highlights the different data types possible on Power BI, shows you how to arrange data in Power BI, exploit tables, use calculated columns, and how to add measures to your data model. It also offers a little on DAX language.

The flow of the book is designed for the readers to follow and apply the instructions given as they are reading along. The book is full of practical tutorials and examples that stimulate understanding in readers. This approach is enlightening and exciting because it will create a classroom-like environment for the reader and encourage the reader not only to visualize but also actualize the step-by-step form of instructions given in the book.

Chapter One

Introduction to Power BI

Microsoft Power BI is a Self-Service Business Intelligence (BI) platform that delivers tools for analyzing, collecting, sharing, and visualizing data to its users. For new users accustomed to using Excel's environment, performing actions on Power BI is not so difficult and requires just a little bit of training.

There are two different versions of Power BI available depending on the payment plan and its use;

- **_Power BI Desktop_**: a free version designed for small scale business owners

- **_Power BI Plus_**: a paid professional version available to its users after payment of a monthly subscription fee. The payment plan comes in two packages depending on the number of users able to create and consume contents. Power BI Pro allows users to create contents and share with other users. It comes at a monthly rate of $9.99 per user that has access to the content and edits. Power BI Premium allows a user to license the contents created and stored in the premium account. Only the creator of the content can edit, the other users only have access to view it. The price of the package varies depending on the number of users allowed to view the content.

Power BI is available for download on Android, iOS, and Windows devices. You can download it from any of the authorized platforms such as *Play store* for Android and website for Microsoft.

Who are the People Using Power BI, and Why?

It is commonly used by data scientists, data analysts, BI professionals, department representatives, and decision-makers in organizations.

Management executives, department representatives, and decision-makers use Power BI to develop reports and make predictions that improve sales and marketing strategies of an organization. Department representatives primarily utilize the tool to observe how individual employees and the department as a whole are reaching and advancing towards the organizational goals.

Power BI can also be used by people without any analytical background (when necessary) to create reports. With Power BI, they can connect separate data sets, clean and transform the data into a model, and construct charts or graphs to visualize the data.

Important Features of Power BI

The first time Power BI was released in 2011, it was called Project Crescent. The renaming occurred in 2013, and it was rebranded as Power BI for Microsoft Office 365. The original version was based on features present in Power Query, Power Pivot, and Power View. Eventually, it was released as a separate product in 2015 and stood apart from the other tools. Microsoft updates Power BI every month, and every time they update Power BI, it comes with new and exciting features. Some of those features include;

- Quick Insights

- Artificial Intelligence

- Hybrid deployment support

- Cortana integration

- Common data model support

- Customization

- Integration APIs

- Modeling views

- Self-service data preparation

The features that are essential for your tutorial will be explained in the appropriate chapter in the book.

How to Download Power BI

This book is a manual on how to operate Power BI. What do you need a manual for if you don't have the equipment yet? So, your first mission is to download Power BI, and a few worksheets and databases to get started. You may use the online version of Power BI, but for effective learning, it's better to use offline resources that are available to you anytime. To download the offline Power BI Desktop, carry out the following steps;

- Visit the Power BI Desktop website.

- Click on the "Download Free" button on the homepage

- Select your language of choice and click "Download."

- Select the files to install and click "Next." The file will begin to download on your PC.

- Install the .exe files with your package installer and launch the program.

- Log in to your Microsoft Office account.

Getting Acquainted with Power BI

To fully understand the process and enhance the learning process, a scenario will be created. The scenario involves Mike Edwards, a budget manager at Enigma industries. The company produces and sells cigars in several countries through local retail shops and online stores. In each of the countries, the product is available, the region managers have the responsibility of estimating figures for the yearly budgets of their countries. When this was done, Mike's continues the job by combining all the different budgets and create a bigger budget for his bosses. Mike intends to create a 2019 budget for Enigma by compiling all the budgets of the regions. A colleague informed him of Power BI's ability to give insights on data and simplify his work. He was amazed and promised to try it out. Mike Edwards just downloaded Power BI. He's never used it before, but he has created several budgets with Excel.

NB: This book assumes you know your way around Excel to a certain degree.

NB: Power BI is not only used for budgeting; this is just a scenario designed to show you how to use Power BI to create a sophisticated report. Follow and replicate the steps Mike takes to acquaint himself with Power BI as this is also his first time using the tool. Your purpose for using Power BI may not necessarily be budgeting so don't bother yourself with the complexities involved in creating a budget, just absorb the steps he took on Power BI to achieve his goal.

Power BI Desktop Options

Like you, Mike Edwards just downloaded Power BI, and he is running the application for the first time. The first thing he notices is the Power BI splash Screen which prompts him to "Sign in" his Power BI account. There is the pop-up menu on the right side of the screen that seeks to give him more information on Power BI. The options available are:

- *What's New-* which gives information on the latest updates and changes made to Power BI

- *Power BI Blog-* which redirects the user to the blog dedicated to Power BI

- *Forums-* which takes the user to the community created for Power BI users to interact and ask questions

- *Tutorials-* this option provides information on how to carry out basic steps on Power BI

Since Mike is not interested in any of the options given, he clears the menu by clicking the "X" symbol at the top of the menu. He proceeds to *Sign in* with his Microsoft 365 Office account.

He uses his work email to register and sign in as Power BI does not allow personal emails like "Mikeedwards@yahoo.com or Mikeedwards@gmail.com."

NB: The preferred email format allowed is
"*Mikeedwards@enigma.com*"

Once he signs in, he is directed to a blank Power BI Window (environment). Here, he notices the dashboard canvas, the Power BI ribbon at the top of the screen, the view type at the top left side of the screen under the ribbon, the page selector at the bottom left side of the screen, and the visualization properties and field lists at the right side of the screen. Generally, the environment is simple and organized for easy access. The functions of each the options listed above include:

— **Power BI Ribbon:** These contain the categories of features needed to develop dashboards on Power BI. The categories on the ribbon are:

- File

- Home

- View

- Modeling

- Help

The function of each category will be discussed at the right junction.

— **View Type:** These options allow you to select the page you want to be in view. The options available are

- Dashboard view- screen where the dashboards and reports are created

- Data view- screen where the data calculation takes place

- Relationship view- screen where data from multiple sources are joined together.

— **Dashboard Canvas:** this is the whiteboard that takes up about 80% of the window. Designing of visualizations and dashboards take place here

— **Visualization Pane and Palette:** the pane is the area for filtering and allocation of element attribute. Formatting of prepared visualization also occurs here. The palette contains the sample structure of all the possible visualizations on Power BI. Selection of the shape of a visual takes place here.

— **Fields list:** contains all the fields in the source data that can be used to create a visualization

— **Page selector:** it is used to switch from one page to another

Uploading Data into Power BI

Mike Edwards finds what he is looking for on the Home ribbon, after observing the components of each tab on the ribbon. He was looking for a way to upload the data he has into the software. He sees "Get Data" and clicks on it. This brings up a dialog box, which shows him all the possible places he can import data from. Since the data he has is in Excel format, he selects Excel and clicks "Connect."

Windows Open File dialog pops up, and he selects the location of his data file, in this case, *RegionBudgets.xlsx*. Immediately he opened the file; Power BI started the uploading process.

How to Create your First Visualization

Now that the data is safely imported into the Power BI Desktop, you will be able to create charts, graphs, maps, tables, and any other element available on the visualization palette with your data. Before you proceed to work on the data, you need to understand a few terms that will be used in the course of the book

- **Visualizations:** these are visual representations of the data uploaded into the software. It may occur in the form of *charts, gauges, graphs, maps, matrixes*, basically anything available on the visualization pane. Any of the words italicized can be used interchangeably with visualization in the course of the book.

- **Dashboard:** The dashboard is a canvas that can contain the visualizations created. The user may prefer to create his visualization on multiple dashboards rather than creating all his visuals on a single dashboard. There is no strict rule about it, as long as he understands how he arranged the visuals. Page and dashboard can be used interchangeably, so don't be bothered if a page is referred to as a dashboard. This is because a page contains all the possible visualization, just like the dashboard.

- **Report:** this word refers to the total pages (dashboards) created from a single data source.

- **Datasets:** all the data sources uploaded to Power BI

Now that you understand the words, it's time for Mike Edwards to create his first visual.

Country/Region	Brand	Month	Sale 2016	Sale 2017	Sale 2018	Budget
United Kingdom	Victory	January	23,234.00		1,945.00	416.66
United Kingdom	Victory	February	6,370.00	7,059.00		416.66
United Kingdom	Victory	March	4,352.00			416.66
United Kingdom	Champion	January	12,418.26	5,735.48	1,559.87	3,041.66
United Kingdom	Champion	February	31,770.26		2,937.90	3,041.66
United Kingdom	Champion	March	3,689.85	5,489.23	11,163.94	3,041.66
United Kingdom	Dark Horse	January	1,271.55	3,236.31	9,945.86	7,875.01
United Kingdom	Dark Horse	February	7,372.34	5,995.55	1,303.01	7,875.01
United Kingdom	Dark Horse	March	11,364.07	2,767.32	3,437.26	7,875.01
Germany	Victory	January	6,270.00			1,125.01
Germany	Victory	February	11,790.00		2,072.00	1,125.01
Germany	Victory	March	5,016.00	3,215.00	8,151.00	1,125.00
Germany	Champion	January	6,249.47		719.55	1,250.00
Germany	Champion	February	8,711.52	2,934.00	1,780.00	1,250.00
Germany	Champion	March	22,928.18		559.65	1,250.00
Germany	Dark Horse	January	8,172.92	93.78	6,800.52	4,166.67
Germany	Dark Horse	February	4,672.77	7,585.29	1,707.56	4,166.67
Germany	Dark Horse	March	12,430.38	2,683.39	5,318.82	4,166.67
Germany	Dark Horse	April	9,626.06	241.77	3,324.75	4,166.67
United States	Victory	January	5,016.00		3,492.00	2,500.00
United States	Victory	February	5,794.00		10,336.00	2,500.00
United States	Victory	March	2,508.00	188.50		2,500.00
United States	Champion	January	8,459.46	1,968.69		1,300.00

13

Excerpt of Mike's Data on Excel

The first column in the excerpt shows the countries that sell Enigma's products; the second column shows the brand. From the excerpt above, you will notice that Enigma industries have four brands of cigars

- Victory

- Champion

- Dark Horse

- Victory II (not shown in the excerpt)

The third column shows the month of the year, and its relevance depends on the fourth to the seventh column. The fourth to sixth column shows the sales of the product per month. The seventh column shows the budget allocated to each country for each brand per month.

The fields column highlights each of the columns in the Excel file Mike uploaded.

- Country/region

- Brand

- Month

- Sale 2016

- Sale 2017

- Sale 2018

The country field has a globe symbol in front of it, which means Power BI recognizes the column contains the name of several countries. The fourth to the seventh field has the "Σ" symbol in front of it. This means that Power BI recognizes the fact that the column comprises of only figures.

NB: If Power BI does not recognize the components of your data, it might create a problem for you when trying to create a visual.

Mike wants to create a visual for the sales of each cigar brand per month, but he is quite confused about what to do next, he notices a button on the home ribbon and decides to use it. The button is called "Ask a Question." He clicks the button, and it produces an input box. He types in "create a visual for sales by month." Power BI automatically generates the necessary column from his data. Mike isn't satisfied with just the column, he wants a visual. Being a naturally curious and intuitive person, Mike clicks on the type of visual he wants to create with the columns Power BI generated. He clicks on the "*Clustered Column Chart*" on the visualization pane (to find out the name of a visual on Power BI, hover your pointer on the shape and the name will automatically come up). Alas, a visual is automatically generated on the column Power BI generated.

How did this happen? With Power BI, it is possible to carry out operations by asking questions. The feature that allows this to happen is called **natural language queries**. With this feature, you can ask Power BI to perform operations, in the same manner, you ask your colleague or junior to perform an operation. Not only will Power understand your question (query), it will also suggest meaningful actions it can perform on your data. This feature does not require the user to have any previous skill on Power BI, you just need to have an idea of the type of visuals you want and the feature will help you bring it to life.

To save the visual created, click on the pin button in the top right corner of the visual on the desktop. This will save the visual to your dashboard, and it will be available to you on any device you connect to your Power BI. When you click on the pin button, a dialog box will pop-up about where to store the visual and what to name it. If it's a free Microsoft account, you will only be able to save to existing dashboard. You can name the visual anyhow you like, as long as you remember what the name represents.

How to Create a Visual Manually

Mike needs another visual that shows the total sales of the three different countries on a single chart. Since he wants this on a new dashboard, he went to the page selector and clicked the plus button. This presented a fresh page free of any visual.

He wants a matrix that shows the values to be used for the visualization, so he clicked the matrix symbol on the visualization pane, then he took his pointer to the fields and selected the columns he needed from the data, which was

- Country

- Sales, 2016

To represent the data selected on the matrix, he wanted a *pie chart*. To do that, he selected the pie chart symbol on the visualization pane. Immediately, Power BI generated a pie chart for the data highlighted.

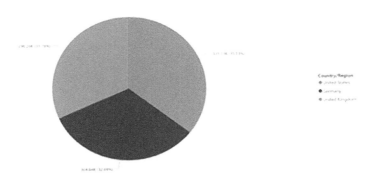

Mike was able to create a pie chart without any previous knowledge of Power BI because the environment was simple and easy to understand. Do you have a particular type of visualization you want to create? Upload your data file now and start creating. Emulate Mike and select the fields you want to use and the type of visual you want to create, it is pretty easy when you do so. If you get confused at any point, do not forget to use the "ask a question" button on the Home ribbon. It will help you create the visuals in your imaginations.

To show the importance of selecting fields, Mike will create another *clustered column chart* but with different fields selected.

- First, he selects the field he wants to use, which are country, month, and sale 2016

- Then he selects clustered column chart on the visualization pane

The combination of the fields and selected visualization created-

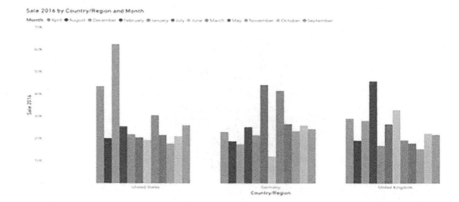

This visualization is different from the first one created because the fields selected are different. When creating your visual, only use the relevant fields for accuracy.

How to Arrange your Dashboard

You have been creating pages to hold new visuals, however, it possible to create all the visuals on a single page. You just need to resize and arrange them.

Resizing a Visual

To do this,

- Click on the visual, it will produce four corners

- Move your pointer to any of the corners

- Adjust until you are satisfied with the size

Arranging a Visual

To do this, you need multiple visuals on the page.

- Resize the visual on the page with the steps above

- When you are done resizing, click on the blank white space on the dashboard to deselect the visual

- Create another visual by selecting the necessary fields and a visualization of your choice.

- Immediately a different visual will be created on the page. Adjust and resize it to your taste.

Quick Facts to Note:

➤ You can create as many visuals as you want on a page, but for a legible and well-arranged dashboard, it is advisable to create only four visuals on a page.

➤ You can change the visualization of any visual on the dashboard with a click on the visualization pane. The same applies to the Fields that make up the visual.

➤ With the simplicity and ease of creating a visual on Power BI, you can easily create four different visuals in less than 10 minutes. Once you have uploaded your data file, your visual is just a click away.

The Interaction of Multiple Visuals on a Dashboard

For this part, you need to upload data to Power BI if you have not been following practically before. Mike's data will be used as an example. Closely observe the following steps performed on Mike's data,

- He clicked on the "+" button in the page selector to create a new page

- He created a slicer by clicking on the necessary field and selecting the slicer symbol on the visualization pane. Slicers can only allow the selection on one field, and in this case, it was "brand."

- He resized the visual till it was about one-fourth of the page

- He created another visual, this time it was a clustered column chart using the fields:

    - Brand

    - Country

    - Sales, 2016

- He resized it to fit the right side of the screen beside the slicer on the dashboard. With this, half of the dashboard is occupied.

- He then created two more visuals, an ArcGIS map, and a matrix. The matrix was created with the same fields as the clustered column matrix while the map is similar to the slicer and only allowed the selection of one field, which was country.

- He resized both visuals to fit the bottom half of the dashboard.

In general, the dashboard he created looks something like this:

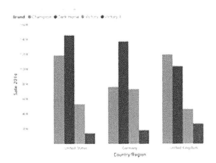

To see the interaction between the four visuals created, Mike clicked on the slicer visual and selected one of the brands, for example, Champion. If you were able to get or create a data similar to the one Mike has and performed the actions Mike performed above, you would notice the change that occurs across all four visuals. The clustered column changed to show only the sales of Champion in the three countries, the map didn't change because all four brands were sold in the same countries, and the matrix changed to only include the total amount generated for the sales of Champion brand in all three countries. Check out the difference in the visual below and the visual in the previous image.

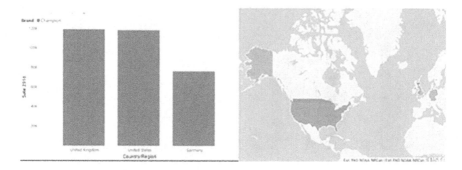

The same type of changes that occurred above will happen again upon the selection of another brand in the slicer.

To check this out, Mike selected Victory II in the slicer and noticed that all the visuals changed to reflect only the properties of Victory II. He selected the other brands available and noted similar changes.

This change does not only happen when an option in the slicer is selected. Out of curiosity, Mike clicked on one of the countries (Germany) on the Map. The visuals changed to highlight the sales that happened in the country. The clustered column chart changed to reflect the sales of each brand in the country and dulled the remaining, the matrix changed to show the total sales the country generated in 2016. There is no change in the slicer because the same brands were sold in the three countries. Check out the visual Mike was able to produce by selecting a country on the map visual:

Brand	Germany	Total
Champion	76,164.02	76,164.02
Dark Horse	137,172.85	137,172.85
Victory	73,267.20	73,267.20
Victory II	18,040.39	18,040.39
Total	304,644.46	304,644.46

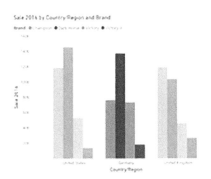

As you can see, clicking on a particular point in a visual may result in a change in all the visuals on a dashboard. Play around by selecting random points to notice the change it will cause, you will learn this way because the next time you are creating a visual similar to this, you will know how to bring to life the kind of dashboard you want.

This shows the dependence and interactivity of dashboards on Power BI. This feature is only a little example of the powerful features Power BI has to offer.

Introduction to Quick Insights

Quick insights, a recent feature added to Power BI with the new update, uses artificial intelligence to analyze a dataset uploaded to Power BI. It utilizes sophisticated algorithms to create interesting patterns and analysis that helps the user understand the report better.

To use Quick Insights, right-click on the report, you want to perform the analysis on your dashboard and select the "Analyze" option. Note that this feature does not work with all visuals. To be able to use this feature, your report has to be in the following visuals;

- Stacked bar chart,

- Stacked column chart,

- Clustered bar chart,

- Clustered column chart,

- Line and stacked bar chart, and

- Line and stacked column chart.

If your report is not in any of the visuals above, the analyze option will not show up when you right-click the report. When the Analyze button is selected, it will bring up another option, "Find where this distribution is different." Click on that option too, and an analysis will be performed on your report. The analysis can be generated within seconds, or it can take longer, it depends on the size of the report.

Mike wants to know if he missed something in the analysis of his report, so he decided to try out the Quick Insights feature. The report he wants to check is the third visual he created, the clustered column chart on the sales of 2016. The analysis of the report took about two seconds, then generated two quick insights, one on sales 2016, the other one on month.

Since Power BI does not have any previous knowledge of your business or its economic condition, it will only interpret the result based on the data uploaded. It cannot imitate your brain's understanding when interpreting the numbers, therefore quick insights should only be used when you want to confirm an analysis, find out if there is something you missed in the interpretation of your data, or to generate fresh ideas. In some cases, the quick analysis insights produce may not be relevant to the purpose of the report, but this is very rare, and if it does happen, it will likely reveal a hidden gem in the numbers causing the deflection from the course.

Formatting of Reports

With Power BI, a user can create multiple visuals in record-breaking time. The visuals are contained within a report. Most times, professionals use Power BI with the intention of generating a report for presentation during a meeting. Just creating a visual is not enough, the report has to be arranged, decorated, and formatted to be presentable to colleagues. Power BI offers a lot of ways to enhance the look and feel of a report resulting in a presentation that will leave your audience in awe of your presentation skills.

How to format a report

The process of formatting a report is not so difficult as Power BI does not require a different technique to format each type of visual. Therefore, you only need to learn a few basic techniques.

- Create a visual.

- Make sure the visual is still selected, then click on the Format icon in the visualization pane. The icon is in the form of a paint roller.

- The format icon will generate a drop-down menu with the following options.

  - General
  - Legend

- X-axis
- Y-axis
- *Data colors*
- Data labels
- Plot area
- *Title*
- *Background*
- Lock aspect
- *Border*
- Tooltip
- Search
- Style
- *Grid*
- Column headers
- Row headers
- Values
- Subtotals
- Grand total
- Field formatting
- Conditional formatting
- Category label
- Word wrap
- Selection controls
- Slicer head
- Items, etc.

Not all the options listed above will come up for one visual. The options that are featured in the drop-down menu depends on the type of visual selected.

NB: It is possible to format multiple visuals at the same time as long as they are of the same type. Two clustered column charts can be formatted at the same time, while a map and a slicer can never be formatted at the same time. The major reason for this is because the formatting pane will generate different format options for a map and a slicer, and this can't be joined together.

Borders

This formatting option is common to all the visuals on Power BI. It creates a boundary around the visual that separates it from other visuals. To create a border

- Click on the visual

- Click on the paint roller symbol

- Scroll down till you see the border option and click on it

- Turn the switch button on

- Select the color of the border

- Adjust the size of the border to your taste

Background Color

The option of a background color is also available to all visuals on Power BI. This option allows a user to change the background color of a visual and differentiate it from others, especially if the visuals are of the same type and have similar data. All visuals have a default background color, white. To change the default color

- Click on the visual that needs a change in background

- Click on the format icon (paint roller)

- Scroll down to back-ground color

- You do not need to switch it on as it is already on, all you need to do is to select a color from the palette and adjust the transparency until you are satisfied.

Titles

While the title formatting option is not available to all visuals, it's quite relevant to the message and delivery of some. You can use the automatically generated title of some visuals based on the selected fields, or you can adjust it to a title of your choice. To change the default title of a visual

- Click on the visual

- Click on the format icon in the visualization pane

- Scroll down to the title option, switch it on if it isn't

- From the drop-down menu created, type in the new title you want, the color of the title, the background color of the title ribbon, the font, alignment, and the size of the title.

Grid

This option is particularly used for visuals containing rows and columns, such as table and matrix. The grid option adds lines (gridlines) to separate the values in a table visual. To create a grid

- Select the visual you want to grid

- Click the format icon

- Scroll down to the grid option

- You have two options, a vertical grid and (or) a horizontal grid

- For the vertical grid, select the color of the grid

- Adjust the size of the text in the visual

- Adjust the outline weight (thickness of grid)

- Select the row padding and the image height.

- For the horizontal grid, there are two additional options of "horizontal grid color" and "horizontal grid thickness."

NB: You can activate both types of grid, but you have to do it one after the other. Finish filling in the requirements of the first one before switching to the other type of grid off.

Data Colors

This is available to all visuals with a color. The option allows the user to decide what color is best to represent the data. Giving data a color makes it different from other data in the visual, and during a presentation, it will be easy to identify a particular data point. To change the color of a data on Power BI;

- Click on the visual

- Click on the format icon in the visualization pane

- Scroll down till you see data color, it will generate a drop-down menu which contains all the default color of your data.

- Click on the group of data whose color you want to change and click on your desired color from the palette. Automatically the color of the data will change in the visual.

There are many more formatting options available on Power BI, the ones mention above are just the basic options that you can adjust in minutes. If you want to explore other format options, create each type of visual on the visualization pane, and adjust the format options available to find out their uses. This should only be done for practice visuals as it may not end up in a visual that is presentable. The only thing you will gain from such a visual is the knowledge of what the formatting option does and how to apply it.

Modifying a Report

You already know how to create a report, now you need to know how to manage and modify it. This will involve the creation of new pages, the renaming of pages, the deletions of pages, the moving of pages, the duplication of pages, and scrolling through numerous pages. The pages on Power BI are much similar to those on Excel, the way Excel users can separate data on different pages, Power BI users can also separate visuals on different pages.

How to Create a Page

You already learned a method on how to do this in *The Interaction of multiple visual on a dashboard.* If you didn't catch the method;

Method 1: Click on the plus button in the page selector corner to create a new page. The page selector is on the bottom left corner of the screen.

Method 2: Click the New Page button on the Home ribbon to create a blank page. The ribbon is at the top of the screen.

It's not very difficult to create a page, is it?

How to Rename a Page

To be able to differentiate between pages easily, they need to have a unique name. To rename them from their default name which is the page number,

- Double click on the tab with the page name, the default page name will be highlighted

- Type in the name you desire

- Press Enter. Click on a blank space in the dashboard to confirm your changes. If the name of the tab remains as the one you typed in, the renaming was a success.

How to Delete a Page

This should only be done when the page is no longer relevant to prevent the loss of valuable information. To delete a page.'

- Hover your cursor on the tab of the page, it will produce an "X" symbol after a few seconds. Click on the X to delete the page

- Clicking the symbol will generate a dialog box, which will warn you of the danger of deleting the file. If you still want to delete, click the Delete button in the box. All the visuals and data on the page will automatically be removed without a trace.

How to Move a Page

This is done to change the default arrangement of a page. By default, a page is arranged in the order of creation, to change the natural order,

- Click on the tab you want to move

- Hold down the tab and drag it to the position you want it to stay.

It does not take blood and sweat to move a page, it can be done in two seconds.

How to Duplicate a Page

If you want to reuse the template and background of visuals you already created on a page, you don't need to start the process all over again. Just copy the entire page and adjust it to what you want. To duplicate a page

- Hover your cursor over the tab of the page you want to copy

- Right-click on the tab, it will generate a few options. Click on the Duplicate Page option. An identical copy of the page you selected will automatically be created.

- You can also duplicate a page by clicking on the New Page button on the Home ribbon.

How to Scroll through Pages on Power BI

It is very stressful to scroll through pages one by one, especially when you have a report with numerous pages. Just like on Excel, you can access a page on Power BI by clicking on the tab. You can also use the scroll button in the page selector corner to move between pages very fast. There are two scroll buttons in the page selector corner, each button has an arrow facing away from each other. The direction of the arrow shows the direction it will move.

Chapter Two

Sharing the Dashboard

Mike Edwards still has a long way to go with his budget. With the skills he learned in chapter 1, he was able to create a dashboard on the first round of analysis. For the next stage of the report, he needs to involve other members of his budget team. Depending on the feedback he receives from his colleagues, he will be able to advance to the next stage with his budget. This chapter will you, the reader, how Mike was able to share his dashboard with his colleague using the in-built features of Microsoft Power BI.

How to Invite a User to View a Dashboard

The first person Mike wants to share his dashboard with is his partner, Perri Johnson. He was able to do that with the following steps

- He opened his Power BI desktop application.

- He clicks the "Share" button on the Home ribbon. The button is located at the extreme right side of the ribbon, directly under the "Publish" button.

NB: The share feature is only available on paid accounts, users with free accounts will not be able to share access to a dashboard.

- Clicking the share button generates a dialog box. The dialog box has two tabs, one is named Share and the other Access.

The Access tab shows the people that already have access to the dashboard. When Mike clicked on the tab, only his name was on the list, and it was tagged "Owner." On the Share tab, he saw an input box for the email address of the recipient. Under the email box, he saw another input box for an optional message to the recipient. Below both boxes were the permission boxes, which allows him to choose the activities the recipient of the access can perform. The three permissions available include

- Permission to share the report to other users

- Permission to create new content using your datasets (this permission was not included before, it came with the latest update on Power BI)

- Permission to receive email notification about details of the report.

The type of activities the user can perform is left to you, in this case, Mike.

- Mike inputs Perri's email address as Perrijohnson@enigma.com. Power BI did not allow him to input the address in full before it automatically generated Perri's email address. This is because Perri is a registered member of Enigma industries, and Power BI has access to the email addresses of all workers in the domain.

NB: It is possible to share the report with people that are not members of the organization, and it is also possible to share with more than one person at a time.

- Mike added an additional message to inform Perri about the progress of the report and the type of feedback he needs on the report.

- The last item on the Share tab is the URL (website link) of the report.

Perri will receive an email containing the link and message from Mike. If Perri is already a user on Power BI, she will be directed directly to the report, but if she is not a user, she will have to register and create an account to gain access to the report.

NB: You can also send the reports to users outside your organization with the same steps listed above. Power BI will recognize the fact that company email does not belong to your organization and will point it out to you. Ignore the warning and continue with the process. Once the user receives the email, he/ she will be able to access the report.

Another way to share your contents with users outside your organization is to publish the report to the web. The publish button is directly above the share button. Click it and publish the report on the web. This feature converts the report into a web link. The major disadvantage of this method is that anyone with a working internet connection and the address of the link can access it. There will be no restriction for the viewing of the report. This method involves the exposure of delicate company information to the general public, so do not use this method unless your organization authorized the publishing of this report.

How to Create a Workspace

Perri has approved the report and has adjusted it in the relevant places. The report is now ready to be viewed by your teammates (the budget managers of each country that sells Enigma's product).

Mike doesn't want to share the report separately to each team member because there are more than 20 people on the team, and each of them will have different editing ideas. Sending the report to them separate will cause a clash of ideas and several misunderstandings. Mike reasons that if each of them has access to a single report at the same time, they will be able to combine ideas and generate a better report within a short period of time.

Before Mike joined Power BI, he heard of a feature called Group Workspace that allows multiple users to edit a single report at the same time and leave messages for each other on the changes they made. Mike was able to access this feature with the following steps:

- He opened the Power BI application on his PC

- He clicked on the "Workspace" option on the navigation pane

- The option generated a menu that had an input box, which served as a search engine for workspaces and a button named "Create A Workspace."

- Mike clicked on the button. This will automatically generate a dialog box. The dialog box instructed him to name the workspace, provide a description for the workspace, and upload a picture for it (optional).

- When he was done filling in the dialog box, he clicked save to finish.

A welcome screen was displayed for the new workspace. Mike named his workspace Budget 2019, therefore the welcome screen displayed "Welcome to the Budget 2019 workspace." To upload a file to the workspace, he clicked the get files button on the welcome screen.

Mike found that it was impossible to transfer reports from his dashboard to the workspace. Power BI does not allow the transfer of reports from dashboards to workspace. Mike would have to recreate the report Perri adjusted on the workspace. Regular users of Power BI create group files on the workspace instead of their personal dashboard to prevent the loss of time involved in recreating a report.

Within minutes Mike was able to replicate his old report due to the ease and simplicity of working on Power BI. The next item on the list is to add members to the workspace, he was able to do that in the following steps:

- He clicked on the workspace menu

- From the menu generated, he left clicked the three inverted ellipses beside the Budget 2019 Workspace. This generated another menu.

- The had two options

    - Workspace Settings

    - Workspace Access

- Mike clicked on the Workspace Access button.

- On the dialog box generated, Mike saw his name as the owner of the workspace. He also saw an input box that allows him to input the email address of his coworkers.

- In the second box, he clicked the category the owner of the email fell into. The four categories include

    - Admin

- Member

- Contributor

- Viewer.

- When he was done with both boxes, he clicked the "Add" button. He kept repeating the process until all 20 members of the team were added.

NB: Only users with paid accounts can create workspaces, it's not allowed on free accounts.

You can restrict the activities of users on your workspace by placing them in the right category. For example, Mike wants all 20 team members to be able to edit the report, hence he registered all the team members in the contributor category.

How to Share a Report on Mobile Devices

For any reason, you may want to view your Power BI reports on your phone or tablet. In Mike's case, he wants to get advice from a close friend. After office hours, Mike met up with his friend Steven at a restaurant. Steven is the budget manager of a company that sells electronic products. During their conversation, the budget Mike was making came up, and he wanted to show Steven some of the visuals he created. Since he wasn't with his laptop, he had to access it on his phone. With the following steps, Mike was able to access his reports,

- He downloaded and installed the mobile version of Power BI from the authorized store. Play Store for Android and iTunes for Apple

- He signed in to his account on the app.

After signing in, he was able to access all the visuals he created on his dashboard. He was able to access the report because he was already signed in on his Power BI Desktop. It's possible to use the desktop version without signing in, but as it says on the splash screen when you first launch the desktop app, to get the most out of the software you have to sign in.

The mobile reports are not editable and have no interactive functions. Basically, the app is only good for viewing and accessing the reports on the go.

Chapter Three

Loading Data from Different Sources

efore you can create a report or perform analysis on Power BI, you need to load your data into the software. The data may be from different sources and exist in different formats. Whatever or wherever you get your data from, you have to access it, restructure it, clean it up, and sometimes join separate data from different sources together before you can create a data model for dashboard and reports. The beauty of Power BI is that you can do all of this on the Power BI Desktop without employing the use of other data structuring tools and software.

Power BI Desktop will help you discover, load, clean, and modify your data, that's one of its area of specialty. With the app you will be able to achieve the following;

- **Data discovery**: Discover numerous data sources containing possibly useful data. The sources may be from private or public domains.

- **Data loading**: Once you have selected the source of your data, upload it to Power BI Desktop for restructuring and shaping.

- **Data modification**: Adjust, filter, and clean the data until it is presentable and workable.

- *Data shaping*: Combine all the data you uploaded (if you uploaded more than one) to create a unified data model.

In most cases, the four steps above are not usually carried out individually and may be blended into a single process. It is possible that you may have cleaned and structured the data before you loaded it into Power BI; in that scenario, you don't need to bother yourself with the process all over again.

Power BI Desktop Query Editor

In Chapter 1, there was a brief tutorial on how to upload an Excel file to Power BI Desktop, however, this chapter will help you take your limited uploading skills to the advanced stage. The chapter will teach you how to upload your data into the Query Editor before uploading it directly to your workspace. With the Query Editor, you will be able to adjust, filter, and cleanse the data before you start creating reports. If your data is clean, you can jump the process and start creating your own data model. The Query Editor feature will be fully discussed in the next chapter.

The Different Data Sources Allowed on Power BI

Power BI allows you to upload and manipulate data from different sources. The sources include;

➤ Database,

➤ Files,

➤ Online services,

➤ Azure, and

➤ Other.

NB: Microsoft is constantly updating and adding new features to Power BI, by the time you are reading this book there may be additional sources available, sources that are not mentioned in this book.

File-Based Data Source

Power BI can access data located on a file in your system. It can even upload an entire folder if needed to access the data. The type of file sources readable by Power BI are:

- Excel – it can read Excel files created in the 97 to 2016 format.

- CSV (comma-separated-format) – these are text files that follow the CSV format

- XML – these are XML files written in a format readable by humans

- Text- general .txt files

- Folder – an entire folder can be uploaded if it contains files readable by Power BI

- SharePoint – connects to the SharePoint folder and upload files in it

- Microsoft Access – connects to the Access folder and upload files in it

- JSON – Power BI can extract data from a .json file

NB: Power BI classifies Microsoft Access as a database source, but for this book, we will treat it as a file, not some a database on some server.

How to Load a CSV Data File

The first thing you have to do when dealing with a CSV is to open the file outside Power BI and determine what needs to be done on the file. If it is arranged and workable, you can load it directly into Power BI but if it still needs some polishing, consider loading it into Query Editor first. The following steps will show you how to load the contents of this file to Power BI and Query Editor

❖ Open the Power BI Desktop App on your system.

❖ Exit the splash screen

❖ Click the "Get Data" button on the Home ribbon. As you know, the act will generate a dialog box

❖ Select "File" among the options given

❖ From the categories of files acceptable click "Text/CSV."

❖ To leave the get data dialog box click "Connect." This will generate the Windows Open dialog box

❖ Find the location of your .csv file. Select it and click "open."

❖ On the dialog box generated after clicking open, there will be a sample of the file you want to upload, and below the sample, there will be three options to select from- Load, Edit, and Cancel.

▪ Cancel – you already guessed what this does, it cancels the entire actions you performed from clicking the Get Data button.

▪ Load – this loads the file directly into Power BI for use

- Edit – this option loads the file into Query Editor for editing.

The choice of the option to click on rests on your shoulders, but for the purpose of explaining how to load .csv into Query Editor click "Edit."

- ❖ On the Query Window, you will be able to add another source and to perform all the necessary edits for the file. When you are done editing, click "Close and Apply" on the Home ribbon. This will close the Query window and take you back to the Power BI Desktop data window.

NB: The process to upload a .txt (text) file is identical to that of CSV. Though they have their little differences, they can be accessed in the same manner.

How to Load an XML Data File

As you probably know since you are using it, an XML file comprises of text formatted in a specific way. To load an XML file into Power BI or Query Editor;

- ❖ Click the "Get Data" button on the Home ribbon. This will generate a Get Data dialog box

- ❖ Select "XML" among the options given

- ❖ Click "Connect" to leave the dialog box

- ❖ On the Windows dialog box generated, find your XML file and click "Open."

- ❖ A navigator dialog box will open, and you will be required to select the dataset you want to load. To choose a dataset, click on the checkbox beside the name. The contents of the selected dataset will be displayed on the right side of the dialog box.

NB: An XML file can contain multiple datasets at once. Power BI allows the user to choose the dataset he wants to upload at that time, meaning only a part of the file may be uploaded at the end of the process.

Note that not all data files will be like XML which allows you to load multiple datasets at once.

❖ Until a data set is chosen, the Load and Edit button will be disabled. After choosing a dataset, you can either click Load, Edit, or Cancel.

❖ Whatever option you choose (except Cancel) when the process is done, you will land on the Power BI Desktop data window. You will be able to access the datasets uploaded in the Fields column on the left side of the screen.

How to Load an Excel Data File

This is the most popular type of data file uploaded to Power BI, most users of Power BI are also professional Excel users. The followings step will cover how to load an Excel file into Power BI;

❖ To take a shortcut from the normal process, click on the small triangle button directly below Get Data.

❖ From the small menu generated, click Excel

❖ Locate the file you want to upload and click Open.

❖ Like XML, Excel can contain multiple datasets at once. Click on the dataset(s) you want to upload to enable the Load and Edit button.

- ❖ Edit the file in the Query Window by clicking Edit or access the file immediately on Power BI by clicking Load.

- ❖ The datasets selected can be accessed in the Fields column on the right side of the Power BI Desktop data window.

How to Import Queries and Models Created in Excel to Power BI

Since the majority of Power BI users have experience in using Excel to create data models, Microsoft designed a way for the users not to lose the data and start again by allowing them to import their worksheets and Power View dashboards from an Excel file into Power BI. The transfer of data from Excel to Power BI is quite easy and can be achieved with the following steps;

- ❖ Open your Power BI Desktop app and exit the splash screen

- ❖ Click the File tab on the ribbon

- ❖ From the drop-down menu created, click "Import."

- ❖ From the options listed in the import menu, click "Excel Workbook contents." This will generate the Windows Open dialog box

- ❖ Locate the file containing your Power Pivot and Power View data and double click on it to open.

- ❖ Once you open the file, Power BI will display a message while importing the file. The message basically states the following

  - o Power BI does not work directly with Excel workbooks, so it will only extract the items in the file that are compatible with Power BI's operating system.

- o From the data imported from the Excel file, Power BI will create a different file which contains the compatible items

- o The importing and file creation process will take a few minutes

Under the message, there are two buttons "Start" and "Cancel." Click on Start to begin the import process

❖ You will be able to see the progress of the importing process. Once the process is completed, Power BI will display the summary of the items imported. When you are done checking the items that successfully imported, click Close to exit the summary dialog.

How to Load a Windows Access File or Database

The reason for classifying MS Access as a file-based data source is because the data source has to be present as a file on your system before you can access it. MS Access databases can contain hundreds of tables and worksheets, which are accessible to Power BI Desktop users. You don't even need to install Access on your system before you can access it with Power BI Desktop.

To import an MS Access file to your Power BI Desktop, carry out the following steps,

❖ Open your Power BI Desktop app and exit the splash screen

❖ Click on the Get Data button on your Home Ribbon

❖ From the menu generated, click "More." This will generate another list of options

❖ From the options generated, click "Database."

❖ From the types of database listed, select "Access."

❖ After selecting Access, click "Connect" to generate the Windows Open dialog box.

❖ On the Windows open dialog box, locate the Access file on your system. When you find the file, click on it and press "OK."

❖ The navigator dialog will automatically generate all the tables and queries present in the file, click the checkbox beside the datasets you want to upload. When you are done, click "Load." To differentiate between the types of data, the navigator dialog box uses two symbols

- A table

- Two windows on top of each other.

The table represents Access tables while the windows represent Access queries.

How to Load a JSON Data File

Using a JSON data file is a relatively new way of storing large amounts of data in a small file. Most JSON files are small in size but can contain millions of data at once. JSON is an acronym for JavaScript Object Notation. To import a .json file into Power BI and Query Editor, carry out the following steps,

❖ Click the "Get Data" button on the Home ribbon. This will generate a Get Data dialog box

❖ Select "JSON" among the options given

❖ Click "Connect" to leave the dialog box

❖ On the Windows dialog box generated, find your .json file and click "Open."

❖ The file will be transferred directly into the Query Editor. In the Query Editor, the file will appear as a *list* of records, and on top of the file, there will be a List Tools Transform ribbon. On the ribbon, click the button named "To Table." This will generate the To Table dialog box.

❖ Below the options listed in the To Table dialog box, there are two button-OK and Cancel. Click the OK button to convert the lists in the .json file to tables. The dialog box will close.

❖ Back in the Query Editor, the *list* of records will change to *column* of records. Beside the column header, a button will appear. The button has a symbol on it, two curved arrows going in opposite directions. Click on the button.

❖ The button will generate a small dialog box. In the dialog box, uncheck the option (box) that states, "Use original column name as a prefix." Close the dialog box by pressing "OK."

The .json file will then appear as a standard dataset with the columns named appropriately and containing the right data. A .json file cannot be uploaded directly into Power BI without editing it in the Query Editor. If you upload it directly, you won't be able to access your data, and any analysis you perform will give false results.

How to Load an Entire Folder into Power BI

Eventually, you will want to upload more than one file at once, probably a hundred. The thought of having to upload each of them one at a time is a discouraging thought. Power BI has a method of getting data that simplified the entire process, it allows the entire contents of a folder to be uploaded at once. However, before the folder can be loaded, it has to fulfill the following requirements

✓ The files in the folder have to be of the same type. This means that if you want to upload a hundred files present in a folder, the hundred files can either be Excel or XML, not XML and Excel. If the folder contains more than one type of format, the importing process may not be a success.

✓ The data in the files have to be arranged in a similar format.

✓ All the files have to be in a single folder, you cannot upload more than one folder at once.

To import an entire folder into Power BI,

❖ Open a new Power BI file. To do that, click on the File tab on the ribbon and select "New." A blank file will be created.

❖ You must know the drill by now. Click Get data, click File, select Folder, and then close the dialog by clicking Connect.

❖ After Connect, the folder dialog box will be generated. As you can see, it is different from the Windows open dialog box. In the folder dialog box, click Browse to find your file. When you find your file, click on it, and you will be directed back to the folder dialog box.

❖ Once you are sure you have the right file, click "OK." The contents of the file will be displayed in the navigator dialog box.

❖ Click Edit to take the files to Query Editor, Load to take the files directly to Power BI, and Cancel to stop the entire process. Now there is another option that makes importing folders different from others. Click "Combine" to join all the individual files into one. This is the reason why the files had to be of the same format, and its contents had to have the same structure.

❖ If you click on Combine button, it will generate a pop-up menu. On the menu, click Combine and Load. This will generate the combine files dialog box. In the box, select the sample file to be used to order the combination of the files.

:. The combined file will be structured in the format of the sample file. It's best to have all the file ordered in the same manner because using this method may scatter the data in the file. Note that there is a "Skip files with errors" option at the bottom of the box, the option is to command the machine to skip files that are not in the same format or order as the sample file.

❖ Click OK to start the combination process. Once it is done, the combined file will be loaded into Power BI Desktop.

How to Load Selected Files in a Folder

If you are not interested in loading all the files in a folder into Power BI Desktop, Power BI provides you with the option to connect the folder to the Desktop without actually loading all the files in the folder. To connect the contents of a folder to Power BI Desktop, carry out the following steps;

- ❖ Open a new Power BI Desktop file

- ❖ Click the Get Data button on the ribbon

- ❖ Click File, select Folder among the options generated, and click Connect.

- ❖ Locate the folder you want to connect in the dialog box generated and click OK

- ❖ This time around, instead of clicking Combine among the options generated, click Load. The paths to the files in the folder will be listed in the Fields column of the new Power BI Desktop file.

How to Create your Own Data on Power BI Desktop

Sometimes the data you need may not be available on a file. Power BI developers added a feature in one of its updates that catered for this need. The Feature allows you to create your own data directly on Power BI. Imagine you already loaded some datasets into Power BI and you're about to start creating a report, but in the process of creating your first visual, you realized that a necessary dataset is missing from the files loaded and the file containing the data is not on your system. What are you going to do then, if you can't work on the other data without that dataset and you know the contents of the file, you just need to find a way to get it into Power BI Desktop? No need to head over to Excel, Access, or any other Platform to create your data, Power BI Desktop has got you covered.

Creating your data on Power BI Desktop is easy just carry out the following steps,

- ❖ On the ribbon at the top of the screen, click Enter Data. It is two buttons away from "Get Data."

❖ A dialog called "Create Table" will be generated. In the dialog box, input the name of your dataset in the box below and fill in the details of your data in the rows and column provided. If you need more rows, click on the asterisk "*" symbol at the end of the column and if you need more columns, click on the asterisk symbol at the right side of the column provided.

❖ When you are done filling in the data, click Load at the bottom of the dialog box to import the dataset into the Power BI Desktop mem0ry.

NB: This feature is designed to help out with small amounts of data. If you need to input huge amounts of data; head over to Excel or use a software that can handle huge amounts of data, the "Enter Data" option is for emergency cases where small datasets end up missing, and it is only effective when the user has knowledge of the contents of the missing dataset.

Database Data Source

The world is full of data, and most of them are in databases on the internet. Fortunately, Power BI is able to connect to most of them, even the ones that are not so recognized. This part of the chapter will cover how to import and load data directly from the database or data warehouse into the Query Editor or Power BI Desktop. The chapter may not be able to cover all the possible databases, data websites, and data warehouses, however, it will cover the major ones, and this will give you an idea of how to approach the rest. Let's get on with it.

Relational Databases

The difficulty you will face when trying to load a data file from a relational database won't be from Power BI, rather it will be from the Guardians of the data on such databases. Once you can get through the logins, special passwords, and other security roadblocks, loading the data into the Power BI Desktop becomes easy. This book will not be able to teach you how to pass the guardians, but it will be able to teach you what to do when you pass the guardians.

The various relational database Power BI Desktop can link you to are listed below;

- ➢ SQL Server database
- ➢ Access database (you already know this, it has been covered in the chapter)
- ➢ IBM DB2 database
- ➢ Oracle Database
- ➢ IBM Informix database
- ➢ IBM Netezza
- ➢ MySQL database
- ➢ PostgreSQL database
- ➢ SAP HANA database
- ➢ Sybase database
- ➢ Teradata database
- ➢ Amazon Redshift
- ➢ Impala
- ➢ ODBC data sources
- ➢ OLE data source

You will be able to connect to all the databases listed above and import records of the data tables that you are permitted to access.

How to Import Data from SQL Server

You won't need to install any special software to import the data from the SQL server into your Power BI Desktop. The approach to import the data is direct. The method used here also applies to Oracle and DB2 database. A great advantage of importing from this server is that you will be able to import several table and data files at once. To connect your Power BI Desktop to an SQL Server, carry out the following steps;

❖ Start afresh, create a new Power BI file on your desktop application.

❖ Navigate your cursor to the Home ribbon at the top of the window. On the ribbon, click the small triangle below the Get Data button.

❖ On the menu generated from the small triangle, click SQL server. Immediately, a dialog box for it will pop up.

❖ In the dialog box, there are two text boxes for the server and database. Type the address or name of your SQL Server in the first box. The SQL server does not necessarily have to be personal, it may also belong to your company. Either of them is acceptable.

❖ In the second box, you may enter the name of the database you want to import. This is optional, but to make the process faster, ensure you have the knowledge of the name of the database.

❖ After filling the two boxes, click the Import option below the boxes.

❖ Click OK to end the first stage of the importing process. Another dialog box will pop up on the screen, the SQL Server database dialog box.

❖ The new box generated is going to ask you detail about your access to the website. If your Window login details is authorized to access the server, click the "Use my current details" option. But if you have an alternative way of accessing the server and database, click the other option, which is "Use alternate credentials." This will activate the Username and Password box below the options. Input the authorized username and password into their respective boxes.

❖ Click Connect to start loading the data file. This will generate a Load dialog box, which will show the progress of the file being imported.

NB: If your internet connection is unavailable, and your Windows login details (or typed-in username) is not authorized to access the file, your Connect command will generate an error, and you won't be able to import the file. So make sure your internet is working, and you are authorized to get that file.

❖ When the file is finished loading, the load dialog box will close and give way for the Navigator dialog box. On the Navigator dialog box, click the boxes of the tables you want to import from the database.

❖ Finally, click Load at the bottom of the dialog box to import it directly to Power BI or click Edit to send it to the Query Editor first. You know the drill.

Now you have successfully imported a data file from the SQL server database into your Power BI Desktop. Go ahead and start transforming it in the Query Editor or creating reports if you loaded it directly into the Power BI Desktop. You can apply the same methods above for most of the relational databases, especially Oracle. The major difference is that in the Get Data dialog box, instead of clicking SQL Server, click Oracle or whatever relational database you want to import from.

How to Import Data from ODBC Sources

The reason why this particular relational database requires it's own separate instruction is that it requires you to install a special software before you can begin importing. The software is called Open Database Connectivity, the full meaning of the acronym ODBC. There are different ODBC drivers for different data sources. An ODBC driver written for a particular data source is going to be slightly different from other data sources and cannot be used for any other data source. If you have a data source that requires ODBC, it's best to download the driver that is particular to it. For this part of the book, you will need to install an ODBC driver to be able to carry out tutorial instructions. You can still follow along if you don't wish to install any, but the best understanding comes from practice. Carry out the following activities to import a data file into the Power BI Desktop through from an ODBC source;

❖ Install the ODBC driver of your data source. If your data source requires ODBC drivers, it will have a download link on the website. Download the software based on the processor of your desktop, if your desktop runs on a 32-bit processor, make sure that is what you download and if it runs on a 64-bit processor, make sure you don't download the version for 32-bit.

❖ After the installation, launch the ODBC Administrator app. Make sure you install this software too if you don't have it already.

❖ On the tab generated for the ODBC Administrator App you, click on the System DSN button at the top.

❖ Click the Add button, it's located on the left side of the screen. This will generate a list of all the drivers installed on your system. The driver you installed in the first step will appear on this list, and any other driver you have installed on your desktop.

❖ Select the Driver for the data source you want on the list.

❖ After selecting the driver, click the Finish button. The dialog box for the driver you picked will be generated. Generally, all ODBC drivers have the same interface with little minor changes to distinguish it from others, but the major features of the drivers are usually the same, which is why the following instructions below apply to all ODBC drivers.

❖ On the ODBC driver dialog box generated, click Next. The button will take you to the tab where you will configure your data source.

❖ On the Next tab, fill in the Name and Description of your data source in the boxes provided. When you are done filling the boxes, click Next.

❖ On the new page generated, type the IP address of the database you want to connect to. Click Next when you are done.

❖ On the next page, select the database you want to connect. From this point, the pages that will be generated will be significantly different. Just follow the trend of the previous instructions and input the required information and click Finish, Next, Done, or whatever final button your driver uses.

❖ When you are "Done," the driver for your data source will be installed in the ODBC administrator app. Click OK to exit the software.

❖ You are back to the Power BI Desktop. Open a new file in the application, you will need a fresh start.

❖ By now, you should know the drill. Click the Get Data button, select Others, choose ODBC in the list generated, and finally click Connect to get started.

❖ In the ODBC dialog box generated, there will be a menu box for the data source names. Select the name that matches the driver you installed above.

❖ Click OK at the bottom of the box to select that data source.

❖ In the Credentials dialog box generated, click the Database option. Enter your username and password details in the appropriate box. The requirement of the third box is optional, ignore it if you don't have the details.

❖ Click Connect to get to the next stage.

❖ In the navigator dialog box generated, select the data files you want to import, then click Load or Edit to import the files to Power BI Desktop and Query Editor respectively.

While this entire process may look tiring, remember that you only have to install the driver once. Once it is installed, you can get any file you want easily by clicking on the Get Data button as the first step.

The other databases, data warehouse, websites, and clouds mentioned in the beginning do not require much stress. With the knowledge and experience, you have gained from importing data from the sources explained in this book, you should be able to get the requirements of their importation easily. If you have data on any of data sources not explained, try to import it now as a form of practice.

Chapter Four

Data Transformation

Loading your data into Power BI Desktop is just the beginning of your work. After loading the data, you have to modify, clean, and filter it to make sure it is ready to be used. This chapter will cover the numerous methods and techniques you can use to transform your data. The numerous methods and process can be grouped into four major categories. The categories do not, in any way, define the order the tweaking or editing process goes. The categories are just meant to intensify your understanding of the process.

- **Data transformation:** This category involves the addition and the removals of rows and columns, the renaming of columns, and the filtering of data.

- **Data modification:** This category involves the altering of original data present in rows and columns.

- **Increasing Datasets:** This category involves the addition of more data to data sets. This process involves expansion of an original column into multiple columns.

- **Combining Datasets:** This involves the joining of two or more datasets into a single data pack.

Power BI Desktop Query Editor

This topic was briefly discussed in the previous chapter. Chapter 3 only gave you a little idea of what this feature entails. The full course will be broken down and downloaded for you in this chapter. You already learned how to load data into Query Editor in the previous chapter, but you did not learn how to use it.

It's not all the time a dataset is available in a ready to go format. Most times, they need to be cleaned over and over till it is ready for use. Query Editor helps you achieve this goal directly on Power BI, you don't need to stress yourself by carrying out the editing process in another software. Power BI Desktop offers two options when loading data into the software, you can either load it first in the Query Editor, or you can load it directly for use. Despite offering these two options, it does not really matter whichever you go for when loading the data. Power BI is not strict on which comes first, if you load the data directly and you noticed the need for editing while creating a report, you can easily go the Query Editor window from the Data Window. You can perform the changes you need, then go back to creating to your dashboard. With this feature, Power BI made editing a data set easy and fast.

The editing tools available on Power BI Desktop are quite sophisticated and can rival the tools available on top editing software. The amazing thing is Power BI Desktop offers the tools for free. To access them on another software, you need to pay hundreds or thousands of dollars per year. While the tools are sophisticated, they are quite easy to use as long as you know what you want to achieve on the data.

The files undergoing a transformation in the Query Editor are called *queries*. To carry out a query, you need to select the data you want to use and begin the importation process. If you're not sure whether to perform a query before loading or after loading, the following scenarios should help you decide;

➢ If you are positive the data in question is clean and well-structured, skip the Query Editor process and load it directly into the Power BI Desktop.

➢ Do you have multiple datasets that need to be combined into a single dataset with the same structure? In this scenario, the best option is to load the data into the Query Editor first. You will be able to see the contents of the file and combine them before transferring it into the Power BI Desktop.

➢ Is your data from a database, a warehouse, or an SQL Server? Then you should probably load the data directly into the Power BI Desktop because most of the data imported from there are usually clean.

➢ Does the data need to be filtered? Maybe some parts of the data are unnecessary and may cause confusion while creating the report. If so, head over to the Query Editor first.

➢ Do you need to change the names of some of your columns for easy understanding? Do you need to modify the data to make it more presentable? Then you have to become friends with Query Editor first.

Your situation may be similar or different from the scenarios above, they are just listed to help you decide on what option to pick when importing a data into Power BI Desktop. The more you work on Power BI, the more intuition you will have on what option to choose.

The Power BI Query Editor Environment

You have to get familiar with the environment of the Editor since the entire data transformation process will happen in there. Query Editor's environment is very different from the Power BI Desktop's environment. The main elements of the Query Editor include;

- The four ribbons at the top of the screen and the *File* menu. The ribbons are named

    - *Transform*

    - *Add Column*

    - *View*

    - *Home*

- *Query list pane* which contains the all the files (*queries*) added to the Query Editor. It is found at the left side of the screen.

- The *data window* is the space where the sample of a query is displayed. It is located in the middle of the screen

- *Query Settings,* the pane is located at the extreme right side of the screen. It contains the list of all the transformation performed on the query.

- The *Formula bar* displays the code that performs the transformation. It is located directly under the ribbons at the top of the screen

- The status bar is found at the bottom right corner of the screen. It shows the number of columns and rows in the query, and it also shows the date the query was loaded into the Query Editor.

- The contents of the cell are shown at the bottom left corner of the screen. It states the exact number of rows and column present in the query.

Applied Steps

Beneath the Properties menu on the Query Settings pane, there is a menu called Applied Steps. The menu contains a list of all the possible transformations that can be performed on a query. As a transformation process is carried out, the menu automatically checks the checkbox beside the performed transformation. It is able to detect every little step performed on a query and records it for future purposes. It is a form of recorder that shows you all you've done on the query.

When you click on a box in the Applied Steps menu, the queries displayed in the Data window will change to reflect the effect of the particular transformation the box covers. Each step you perform on the query is named, this allows you to trail your every step in the modification process. The manner in which the steps are named will be discussed when the possible transformation steps are explained later in the book.

The Four Ribbons

You already know the name of the four ribbons present at the top of the Query Editor Window, but you don't know their functions. Each button present on the ribbon will be discussed in this chapter. You don't have to memorize all the functions. You just need to have a general idea of what the buttons do and the button to click when you need to perform a particular modification. You could always refer to this book later on when you need to carry out a transformation you don't know much about. All the buttons and their possible functions will be listed and explained.

Home

Below are the description and functions of all the button present on the Home ribbon as of the last update on August 2019. The ribbons are arranged according to the way they are located on the ribbon.

Buttons	Functions
Close & Apply	This is the first button on the Home ribbon. Selecting this button will save all the changes performed on the query and close the Query Editor window. You should only use this button when you are done with the transformation process.
New Source	This button allows you to add more queries to the one present i the window
Recent Source	This button lists all the queries you have edited on the window recently. It also allows you to open them again in a separate window different from the one you're on.

Buttons	Functions
Enter Data	This allows you to create your own custom-made data in the Query Editor
Data Source Settings	This gives you control over the data sources already connected to the Query Editor
Manage Parameters	Grants you access to modify the parameters defined for the query file
Refresh Preview	This performs a refresh on the sample query
Properties	Shows the basic properties of the query file, such as the size, the name of the file, and the date it was created.
Advanced Editor	Shows the editor of the M language used in data modeling
Manage	Allows you to copy, delete or cite a query
Choose Columns	Gives you the power to select which columns to retain among all the columns available in a query

Remove Columns	Grants you the ability to delete one or more unnecessary columns in the query
Keep Rows	This allows you to choose the number of rows to keep in a query, counting starts at the top of the table.
Remove Rows	This allows you to remove a specific number of rows from the original number of rows in a column. Counting also starts at the top of the table.
Sort	Arrange (sort) the table using a specific column in the query as a sample
Split Column	Divides a single column in the query into other columns after a fulfilling a particular requirement
Group By	Assembles the columns into categories based on the contents of the columns
Data Type	Allows you to choose a data type and apply it to a particular column
Use First Rows as Headers	Gives you the ability to convert the function of the first row in a column. The first row stops being a simple row and becomes the title of the entire column.

Replace Values	This button carries out the search and replace operation in the Query Editor. It only changes the values specified in the search box to the values in the replace box. It won't affect the other values that are not present in the search box.
Merge Queries	This allows you to combine two or more queries together. It joins the columns and adds the values to make a single query.
Append Queries	This allows you to add the data from a previous query to the query opened in the Query Editor. This does not join the column or adds the values as Merge Queries does.
Combine Files	Joins and combine the data from multiple files into a single table. This is possible as long as the files are of the same format, have the same number of columns, and have the same type of data in each column. This is different from the Append query because it does not deal with previous queries, it deals with files.

Transform

The transform is the richest of the ribbons in terms of features and functions. It has about 32 buttons on it, and they all have different functions. The buttons on the transform ribbon can be classified into seven major categories, they are;

❖ *The Table Transformation Buttons:* These are the buttons in charge of the transformation of a table as a whole. They include:

Buttons	Functions
Group By	This button can also be found on the Home ribbon. It assembles the columns into categories based on the contents of the columns.
Use First Rows as Headers	This is also present on the Home ribbon. It grants you the ability to convert the function of the first row in a column. The first row stops being a simple row and becomes the title of the entire column. As you can see, this affects the table as a whole. That's the reason why this button is in this category.
Transpose	This button interchanges the directions of the rows and columns. With this button, the rows become columns, and the columns become rows.
Reverse Rows	This button interchanges the order of a table. The bottom rows become the top

	rows, and the top rows become the bottom. While this might look confusing, the interchange occurs in a specific order, the last become the first, and the first becomes the last. The remaining rows follow that order.
Count Rows	This performs a count operation on the table and automatically replace the data in a row with the number the row falls on in the table.

The Column Transformation Buttons: These buttons are in charge of transforming a column. The buttons can only affect the dynamics of a column. They include:

Buttons	**Functions**
Data Type	With this button, you can select the type of data present in each column. It could be text or numbers.
Detect Data Type	This automatically detects the data type present in each column and uses it to determine the appropriate data type to apply to the column.
Rename	This allows you to change the name of any column in the query.
Replace Values	This button performs the same function as the one on the Home button. It carries out

	the search and replace operation. It changes the values specified in the search box to the values in the replace box. It won't affect the other values that are not present in the search box.
Fill	Copies the content of an entire cell and dumps it into an empty column. You can decide the order it copies the content, it may be from above or from below.
Pivot Column	This button converts the contents of a column into the titles of other columns. This means that each row of a particular becomes the title of different columns.
Unpivot Columns	Performs the opposite of what the Pivot Column button does. It takes the titles of each column in the query and converts it to rows in a single column, while the data present in the columns are merged to become a single column. At the end of the day, two columns are formed- the column for all the titles and the column for the data.
Move	This button can change the position of a column
Convert to List	When clicked the button will convert all the columns in the queries to a list

❖ *The Text Transformation Buttons:* Performs actions that are related to the text in the query. The text transformation buttons are:

Buttons	Functions
Split Column	Divides a single column in the query into other columns after a fulfilling a particular requirement
Format	Formats the text in the columns. Regularizes the use of lowercase, uppercase, and the capitalization of the text. It also removes excess space in the columns.
Merge Columns	This button performs the opposite of what the Split Column button does. It joins two or more columns together to form a single column. It separates the data in the column by placing them on different lines.
Extract	The function of this button is quite complicated. In a way, it limits the number of characters that can exist in a column. After clicking the button, you must specify how many characters should exist in the column. With the button, you can also set a condition that requires each cell in each column begins with a specific character and replace the data in a column with a defined subset of data.
Parse	This button converts the contents of a column into a .json, .xml or .txt format document.

❖ *The Number Transformation Buttons:* These buttons are only corned with the values in the query. Their actions are directed towards transforming the numbers in the table. Buttons in this category are:

Buttons	Functions
Statistics	This performs statistical operations on the values in the columns. The possible operations include the calculating of the total sum of the values, the mean of the values, the median, pinpointing the largest value, the smallest value, calculating the Standard Deviation, performing a count of all the values in the column.
Standards	This button also performs calculations on the values in a column, but unlike Statistics Button the operations performed here are rather basic. It is used to calculate the addition, subtraction, division, multiplication, integer division, and modulus of the values in a column.
Scientific	This is also another button that performs calculations. The calculations here are scientific. Calculations like finding the Square, Raise-to-power, Cube, Square root, Exponent, Factorial, and Logarithm of values in a cell.
Trigonometry	Performs trigonometric operations like finding the Cosine, Sine, Tangent values of each row in a column.

Rounding	This button approximates the values of data in a column. It can either round it up or down depending on the factor specified.
Information	Tests condition of data in a column. The possible results are Even, Odd, Positive, and Negative.

❖ *The Date and Time Transformation Buttons:* Include buttons that are helpful when some of the data in the queries are time-related. The buttons are:

Buttons	**Functions**
Date	This button only works when the values involved are dates. This could be values stating the day, month, or year. It isolates the date element from others in the column.
Time	This button only works when the values involved are related to time. This could be values stating the hour minute, seconds, or nanoseconds. It isolates the time element from others in the column.
Duration	This button takes account of two values and measures the duration, be it in minutes or days. Before this operation can work, the Editor has to recognize the values in the columns as dates and time.

❖ *Structured Column Buttons:* These buttons are only activated during the combination process of two or more queries. They help to structure the combined columns of the queries, they are;

Buttons	Functions
Expand	This button allows you to combine two identical queries together. It joins the columns and adds the values to make a single query.
Aggregate	This button allows you to sum the values of the two queries together. Basically, it performs an expanded function of the Standards button. It adds the numeric values in the columns of two queries and presents it in the current query.
Extract Values	This button converts the values in a column to text and extracts it.

❖ *The Run Scripts Buttons:* Carries out instruction written in machine language. Languages like "R," and many more. There is only one button in this category, it is:

Buttons	Functions
Run R Scripts	Runs instructional codes written in R

Add Columns

This ribbon does not exist just for you to be able to add columns to a query, it can break a single column into multiple columns, and it can add new columns that contain information on date and calculations from existing columns in a query. The Add column ribbon is divided into four categories, namely:

❖ *The inserted column buttons:* These buttons are in charge of adding new columns to a query, they include:

Buttons	Functions
Column From Examples	This button allows you to select an existing column as the sample of how the new column to be created should be. After clicking the button, you will have to select the sample column to begin the process.
Custom Column	This button creates a new column whose contents are custom made from existing columns. The new column is created with a formula that uses variables from existing columns.
Invoke Custom Function	Using this button will require the knowledge of "M" language. After clicking the button, an input box will be generated for the code of the language. When you are done with the code, the interpreter of Power BI Desktop will run the code and apply it to the necessary part of the query.

Conditional Column	This button creates a column based on an existing column fulfilling a particular condition. When a column fulfills the requirements, interpreted values from the column will be added to the new column.
Index Column	This button creates an index column to identify the existing rows. The index column numbers each row in the query with a unique number or roman numeral.
Duplicate Column	The function of this button is pretty basic. It merely duplicates the contents of a column.

❖ *The text column buttons:* The functions of the buttons here are similar to the "Text transformation tool" in the Transform Ribbon. The buttons present in this category are:

Buttons	Functions
Format	Formats the text in the columns. Regularizes the use of lowercase, uppercase, and the capitalization of the text. It also removes excess space in the columns.
Merge Columns	This button joins two or more columns together to form a single column. It separates the data in the column by placing them on different lines.

Extract	The function of this button is quite complicated. In a way, it limits the number of characters that can exist in a column. After clicking the button, you must specify how many characters should exist in the column. With the button, you can also set a condition that requires each cell in each column begins with a specific character and replace the data in a column with a defined subset of data.
Parse	This button converts the contents of a column into a .json, .xml or .txt format document.

❖ *The number column buttons:* The buttons in this category deal with columns that contain numbers in a query. With the buttons, you will be able to manipulate the numbers and perform actions on them. The buttons include:

Buttons	**Functions**
Statistics	This performs statistical operations on the values in the columns. The possible operations include the calculating of the total sum of the values, the mean of the values, the median, pinpointing the largest value, the smallest value, calculating the Standard Deviation, performing a count of all the values in the column.

Standards	This button also performs calculations on the values in a column, but unlike Statistics Button the operations performed here are rather basic. It is used to calculate the addition, subtraction, division, multiplication, integer division, and modulus of the values in a column.
Scientific	This is also another button that performs calculations. The calculations here are scientific. Calculations like finding the Square, Raise-to-power, Cube, Square root, Exponent, Factorial, and Logarithm of values in a cell.
Trigonometry	Performs trigonometric operations like finding the Cosine, Sine, Tangent values of each row in a column.
Rounding	This button approximates the values of data in a column. It can either round it up or down depending on the factor specified.
Information	Tests condition of data in a column. The possible results are Even, Odd, Positive, and Negative.

❖ *Data and time column buttons:* Buttons in this category deal with the columns that contain details on the time and date of an activity. The buttons include:

Buttons	Functions
Date	This button only works when the values involved are dates. This could be values stating the day, month, or year. It isolates the date element from others in the column.
Time	This button only works when the values involved are related to time. This could be values stating the hour minute, seconds, or nanoseconds. It isolates the time element from others in the column.
Duration	This button takes account of two values and measures the duration, be it in minutes or days. Before this operation can work, the Editor has to recognize the values in the columns as dates and time.

View

View is the last column in the Query Editor ribbon but not the least used. While the significant transformation actions take place in the other ribbons, the view ribbon is used to monitor the appearance of queries in the Query Editor. The buttons on the ribbon include:

Buttons	Functions
Query Settings	This button allows you to choose whether the Query Settings column should be visible or not. The Query Settings column appear at the right side of the Query Editor window, and one of the items on it is the Applied Steps list.
Formula bar	This is not really a button, it's more of a checkbox. The checkbox allows you to choose whether or not the formula bar should appear at the top of the data window. The formula bar is the input box where the M language for coding is written.
Monospaced	This is also a checkbox, not a button. It is used to display the text in the query in a monospaced font (Courier).
Show Whitespace	This is the third checkbox in this ribbon. It allows you to decide whether you want to see the whitespace present in the query or not. This checkbox is always clicked by default, if it's not what you want, you have to turn it off.
Go to Column	This button allows you to move your cursor to a particular column in the query. It lists the columns available, you can go to the column by clicking on it. It's a very fast method of shuffling between columns

	in queries with large contents.
Always Allow	This checkbox allows you to turn on parameterization.
Advanced Editor	This button generates an Advanced Editor dialog box which shows the codes of the transformation steps performed on the query.
Query Dependencies	This button shows links and dependencies of the query in the Query Editor.

Transformation Steps in the Query Editor

Now that you know the name and functions of all the buttons in the query editor, you also need to learn how to apply them. While most of them are self-explanatory, you may need help to understand the right instance or the necessary circumstance for a button to be used. This part of the book assumes that you already have a file imported into the Query Editor. At this point, you are no longer a novice when it comes to Power BI, so Mike Edwards and his file problems won't be used anymore in the book. The rest of the book will offer instructions that are designed to help you improve your file transformation skills.

Restructuring the Data in a Query

At the beginning of the chapter, the editing process that happens in the Query Editor was divided into four; Data transformation, Data modification, increasing datasets, and combining datasets. It was also stated at the beginning of the chapter that the classification of the editing process into four categories was not a clear classification and that the classification was just to ease your understanding. It will be easy to categorize the restructuring process of a query under Data Transformation, but data transformation covers a whole lot more. The editing/transformation steps that fall under this heading, they include:

➢ *Renaming of Columns,*

➢ *Reordering of Columns,*

➢ *Removal of Columns,*

➢ *Merging of Columns,*

➢ *Removal of Records, and*

➢ *Filtering of data.*

These processes/steps belong to this heading because they affect the general structure of the data in a query. You will discover more transformation steps in the future.

How to Rename a Column in the Query Editor

The method available to rename a column in the Editor is quite easy to learn and memorize. You can rename a column with the following steps;

❖ Click on the column you want to rename. It does not necessarily have to be the first row in the column, you can click on any part.

❖ Click on the Transform ribbon at the top of the Editor. The default ribbon is the Home ribbon, you will need to click the Transform button in the ribbon to display the buttons on the ribbon.

❖ You are interested in the Rename button on the ribbon. Click on the Rename button, and this will highlight the original name of the column in the first row. Enter the new name of the column into the box.

❖ When are done typing, click the Enter button on your keyboard to save the name.

NB: The moment the name is saved, the ***Applied Steps*** column will have an item on it. The item is called *Renamed Columns*. If you click on the item, it will highlight the name of the column you renamed.

How to Reorder Columns in the Query Editor

In the scenario that the rows in your data are disordered, you can arrange them in the Query Editor of the Power BI Desktop. First, you have to import the dataset into the query editor. After that, you can reorder the columns with the following steps;

❖ Click on the header of the disordered column.

❖ Drag the column to the position you want it to be in, then unclick the column to drop it in that position.

You can also perform this action with a button in the Transform Ribbon;

❖ Click on the column you want to move.

❖ Click on the "Move" button in the Transform ribbon

❖ It will generate a set of options, they are

▪ Left

▪ Right

- To Beginning

- To End

Click on the direction you want the column to move, keep clicking until it reaches your desired position.

NB: The name of this process in the *Applied Steps* column is *Reordered Columns*.

How to Delete/ Remove a Column in the Query Editor

Assume you have a data file with excess and (or) conflicting information on it. Before you can work on that type of file, you need to remove the excess information, so it does not conflict with the data you need to create your reports. To remove a column from a query, carry out the following instructions;

- ❖ Click on the column you want to delete. If you want to delete multiple columns at the same time, Hold Control and click on all the unwanted columns.

- ❖ When the columns are selected, click on the Remove Columns button on the Home ribbon. All the columns will disappear immediately, and *Removed Columns* will become an item on the *Applied Steps* column.

In the scenario that your file is from a database and you only need a few columns from all the columns available in the dataset, Power BI has a separate option for such needs. To only keep specific columns from all the columns available in a query, carry out the following steps;

- ❖ Hold Control and click on all the files you want to keep

❖ Head over to the Home ribbon at the top of the Query Editor, find the Remove button and click the triangle below the button. From the options listed, click remove other columns. Immediately, the unselected columns will be deleted, and an item named Removed Other Columns will appear in the *Applied Lists* column.

How to Choose Columns in the Query Editor

Files obtained from databases usually contain large contents, more than you may need for your report. To prevent the unnecessary columns from showing in the Power BI Desktop and crowding your Fields column, you can select the ones to be displayed. In a way, it is similar to the Remove Other Columns action performed above but, in this case, the columns are not deleted, just hidden away from view and cannot be used to perform any action in the Power BI Desktop. To choose columns to be used to create reports in the Query Editor, perform the following actions;

❖ Click on the Choose Columns button in the Query Editor. It can be found at the center of the Home ribbon.

❖ A "Choose Columns" dialog box will be generated. In the dialog box, there are checkboxes besides all the columns present in the query (data file). Click the checkbox beside the "Select all Columns" option at the top of the list to deselect all the columns.

❖ Then, click the checkboxes of the column you want to work on in the Query Editor and Power BI Desktop. You can search for the columns you want in the search box at the top of the dialog box, and you can also arrange the columns alphabetically to make the selection process easier. Click the

A->Z button beside the search box to arrange the column alphabetically.

❖ When you are done choosing columns, click OK to apply the changes.

Only the columns selected will be available for use in the Query Editor, and finally in the Power BI Desktop data window.

NB: This action will not generate an item in the *Applied Steps* column because the query will be refreshed and only the columns selected will be displayed. Since you haven't performed an action on the new set of columns, there will be no item in the *Applied Steps* column.

How to Merge Columns in the Query Editor

Source data files do not always come in a presentable or refined order. Sometimes data that can exist in a single column may be spread into multiple columns that may or may not have a meaning. Power BI allows its user to adjust files like that to have more meaning. The feature that allows the merging of columns is present in the Query Editor, you can perform the action with the following steps;

❖ Hold Control and click on all the columns you want to merge.

❖ Click the Transform ribbon to reveal all the buttons on it. Click on the Merge Columns button. This will generate a Merge columns dialog box.

❖ Click on the Separator box, it will generate a menu which contains all the possible options you can use to separate the columns. You can choose any separator on the list.

❖ In the second box in the dialog box, input the new name for the merged column.

❖ When you are done filling the two boxes, click OK to start the merging process.

NB:

- There is no limit to the number of columns that can be merged, any number is possible.

- If you don't name the new column in the dialog box, by default, it will be named as "Merged" when created. After creation, you can then rename it with the rename button on the ribbon.

- The order in which you select the columns in the first step is critical. The items in the merged column will be arranged according to the order they are chosen. This means that the first column to be selected becomes the first item to appear in the merged column. Make sure you take note of this fact when selecting the columns to be merged as it will not be possible to change the order when the merged column is created. Once the column is disorganized, you will have to undo the action (Control Z) and start the merging process all over.

- The merging process removes the original columns from the query. Once the columns are merged, you won't be able to perform any action with the old columns. If you still have use for the individual columns, it is best to duplicate them before you merge it.

- In the separator box in the dialog box, there are several separators you can choose from. The options include;

i.   Colon (:)

ii.   Comma (,)

iii.   Equals to Symbol (=)

iv.   Semi-Colon (;)

v.   Space ( )

vi.   Tab (->)

vii.   Custom

The custom option lets you create a unique separator that is different from the ones present on the menu. When you click the custom option, an input box will be generated, and you will be asked to type in the character you want to use as the separator.

- The action generates an item on the **Applied Steps** column. The item is named *Merged Columns.*

How to Select a Specific Column in the Query Editor

In queries with hundreds of columns, moving through the columns one after the other may become tedious after a while. Power BI's Query Editor has simplified this process by creating a quick way to select a specific column with one of the buttons on its ribbon. To select a specific column, carry out the following steps;

❖ The button you need to carry pout this action can be found on the Home ribbon. Find the Choose Columns button on the ribbon and click the small triangle below it. This will generate a Choose Columns dialog box.

❖ In the dialog box, there will be a list of all the columns in the query. The columns will be arranged in the original order they were saved in the query. To arrange them alphabetically for easy surfing, click on the A->Z button beside the search box. Find the column you want to select, click it, and click the OK button at the button to exit the dialog box.

When the dialog box closes, the column you selected will be highlighted.

NB:

- With this method, you can only select one column.

- This action does not generate an item in the Applied steps column since it didn't cause a change in the query.

How to Manage Rows in Query Editor

So far, we've only covered how to manage the columns in a query. It showed how to select, rename, reorder, move, delete, and merge columns. All the actions that were used to manage the columns cannot be applied to rows, it has its own unique set of buttons. There are three basic approaches when it comes to managing rows in a query. They are;

➢ Keeping specific rows

➢ Removing specific rows

➢ Removing blank rows

How to Keep Specific Rows in a Query

In the scenario that you downloaded or imported a file from a database, the file will contain more data than you need. Let's assume you are interested in all the columns and only need a few rows for your report. In that case, you will need to find a way to delete the other rows. You can keep specific rows in a query with the following steps;

❖ Find the Keep rows button on the Home ribbon in the Query Editor. Click on it when you see it. This will generate a menu.

❖ In the menu generated, there are three options available to pick from.

- Keep Top Rows

- Keep Bottom Rows

- Keep Range of Rows

What you pick will determine the type of dialog box that will be generated.

1. If you select Keep Top Rows, a Keep Top Rows dialog box will be generated. In the dialog box, you will see a box, which allows you to input the number of rows at the top you want to keep. This means that if you input 10 in the box, only the top ten rows will be kept.

— When you are done, click the OK button at the bottom of the box to finish the process.

— An item will be generated on the *Applied Steps* column, the item will be named *Kept First Rows*.

2. Selecting the Keep Bottom Rows option will generate a Keep Bottom Rows dialog box. In the input box, you can type the number of rows at the bottom you want to keep.

— When you are done, click the OK button at the bottom of the box to finish the process.

— Immediately an item will be generated on the *Applied Steps* column, the item will be named *Kept Last Rows*.

3. The last option is the Keep Range of Rows option. Selecting that option will generate a Keep Range of Rows dialog box. There are two boxes in the dialog box, the *First-row box* and *the Number of rows* box.

— In the First-row box, input the index number of the first row you want to keep. This is where the counting will start from.

— In the Number of rows box, type in the number of rows you want to keep. The number here starts counting from the row mentioned in the First-rows box. This means if you input 25 in the First-row box and 50 in the Number of rows box, the rows 1 – 24 will be deleted, 25 – 74 will be kept, and 75 downwards will be deleted.

— When you are done, click the OK button at the bottom of the box to finish the process.

— An item will be generated on the *Applied Steps* column, the item will be named *Kept Range of Rows*.

How to Remove Specific Rows in a Query

You already learned how to keep specific rows, now you have to learn how to remove specific rows which is the opposite of keeping certain rows. To keep certain rows in a query, carry out the following steps;

❖ On the Home ribbon, click on the Remove Rows button. This will generate a menu similar to that of Keep Rows.

❖ In the menu generated, there are five options available

- Remove Bottom Rows

- Keep Errors

- Remove Top Rows

- Keep Duplicates

- Remove Alternate Rows

Ignore the Keep Duplicates and Keep Error buttons, for now, click on any of the other options on the menu. It depends on the position of the rows you want to delete. For Remove Bottom Rows and Remove Top Rows, the dialog box generated is identical to that of the Keep Top Rows and Keep Bottom Rows dialog box. Just input the numbers you want to remove then end the process with the OK button. The item generated in the *Applied Steps* column will be named *Removed Top Rows* and *Removed Bottom Rows* respectively.

For Remove Alternate Rows, the dialog box generated is very different from the other options. There are three input boxes in the dialog

- First row to remove

- Number of rows to remove

- How many rows to keep.

Clicking this option is tricky, and it should only be used when you want to create a new set of data from the original query. To use the alternate row option;

— Input the index number of the first row you want to keep in the first box. For example, 10.

— Then input the number of rows you want the editor to remove after the first row mentioned in the box above. For example, 2.

— Finally, type in the number of rows you want to keep to form a new query. For example, 10.

The editor will interpret the instructions given above as a command to alter the query to contain only ten rows. It will take the tenth row as the first row, delete the next 2 rows after the tenth row, save the original thirteenth row (add it as the second row in the altered query), and continue the process of deleting two rows then saving the third until a total amount of ten news rows are created.

Now you can see the reason why the alternate rows option is a tricky process. The new rows formed will be totally different from the original rows in the query. Only use this option when you are totally sure of what the process will achieve.

NB: When the Alternate rows are created, the step will be named as *Removed Alternate Rows* in the ***Applied Steps*** column.

How to Remove Blank Rows in a Query

Sometimes, a data file might contain empty columns and rows. In a bid to clean the file, you have to remove all these unnecessary excesses in the file. To remove the blank rows in a query, carry out the following steps;

❖ On the Home ribbon in the Query Editor, click on the Remove Row button.

❖ On the menu generated in the button, click Remove Blank Rows. This will order the editor to identify and remove all the blank rows present in the query.

On the *Applied Steps* column at the right side of the editor, an item will appear on the list. The item will be named *Removed Blank Rows*.

How to Remove Duplicate Data from a Query in the Query Editor

One of the most annoying situations that can happen when handling a file is having a document with repeated data. Creating a report with such a file will only end badly. Power BI's Query Editor has a feature that identifies repeated entries and allows you to delete them in one go. Sometimes, you may not even notice that a part of the data has been duplicated, this won't matter in the Query Editor as it automatically identifies all the cells containing identical characters. To remove duplicate data entries in your query, carry out the following steps;

❖ Click the top left corner of the table grid. This will generate a pop-up menu

❖ On the menu, click the Remove Duplicate option. This will automatically remove all duplicates and add an item called *Removed Duplicates* to the *Applies Steps* column.

NB: This removal of Duplicate contents is a very risky process, it will delete *all* entries with identical characters. If a single character is different, it will not be counted as duplicate content, so it is pretty accurate in that manner. The reason why it is risky is that it will remove *all* duplicate contents, not just one half, it will remove *all*.

The feature does not allow some of the contents to be saved, all the entries that look identical will be deleted. This is risky cause you may need some of the deleted entries when creating your report.

Before you resort to this method, make sure you delete all the columns and rows in the query you don't need for your report because some cells may contain identical contents and result in the deletion of contents you actually need.

Alternatively, you can check out the duplicated contents before you delete them. To do this, click on the Keep Duplicates option in the table menu. This will show you all the contents that were duplicated in the query. Take notes of all the cells containing duplicate contents that you may still need. Then delete the *Kept Duplicates* item on the Applied Steps list to undo the action or simply press Control + Z. This will take you back to the original query. There you can manually delete the duplicates of the contents you may still need so it isn't deleted along with the other duplicate contents.

Filtering the Data in a Query

As you must know, data files may come with so much unnecessary and irrelevant information. Before you start creating reports on your dashboards, you need to filter all the irrelevant parts of the data. Filtering on Query Editor is much like filtering with a sieve, the menu the column generates becomes the sieve that filters unwanted entries from critical entries. There are two basic tactics employed when filtering a data file, they are;

➢ The selection of specific entries or records

➢ Defining the range of the relevant data

How to Filter Data by Selecting Specific Records

This method allows you to choose the particular records you want to use to create your reports. While this method might be very similar to the Choose Columns feature explained above, it's quite different. With Choose Columns, you will have to select the entire column, but with specific values filtering, you can choose the parts of the columns you want to keep. It does not restrict you like Choose Columns. To filter your data file by selecting specific values;

❖ Click on the small triangle beside the title of the column you want to filter. This will generate a popup menu.

❖ On the second part of the menu, there is a list of all the entries in the column. Click the checkboxes of all the entries you want to keep. All the boxes will be checked by default, simply uncheck the boxes of the entries you don't want to keep.

❖ Click the OK button at the end to finish the process. Immediately, *Filtered Rows* will appear as an item on the **Applied Steps** column.

NB: In the spirit of removing irrelevant data, you can click the *Remove Empty* option on the menu to remove blank rows from the data. It's also part of the filtering process.

How to Filter Data by Defining the Range of Data to be Kept

While selecting the specific rows to keep is more precise, it will become a laborious process, especially when you are dealing with queries that contain hundreds of column. Defining the range of the entries to be kept makes the process easier. You can define the range of the data in a query by;

❖ Click on the small triangle beside the title of the column to generate its menu.

❖ In the menu, there is a search box above the list of all the rows in the column. In the menu, type in the entry you want to keep. When the search results are generated, click the *Select all Search results* checkbox to keep all the entries in that category. You can perform this over and over till all the entries you are interested in are ticked. This is much faster than selecting the entries one by one.

❖ Click the Ok button at the button to initiate the filtering. The same *Filtered Rows* will appear on the **Applied Steps** column.

The filter popup menu can carry out several actions, depending on what you order it to do.

● If the column contains text, a Text filter option will be available. With the option, you will be able to set or exclude the presence of a specific text in the row, set the character the text must begin with, not begin with, end with, not end with, contain, and does not contain. This is as precise as it can get.

● If the column contains numbers, a Number filter option will be available. With the filter, you will be able to specify the exact numbers in the allowed entries and the numbers that must not be in the entry. You will also be able to set a limit for the values of the numbers, whether maximum or minimum (greater than, less than, greater than or equal to, and lesser than or equal to).

● And if the column contains time values, date, minutes, seconds and the likes, a *Date and Filter* option will be available on the menu. With the filter, you will be able to determine the type of dates or times you want to be filtered out and many more.

As it was said above, the filter feature in Power BI is a very powerful tool. It can even weed out air if you set the right parameters. That was a joke!

How to Save all the Changes made in the Query Editor

You can save the changes made in the Query Editor at any time, even when you are not done with the transformation process. To save the changes made, carry out the following steps;

❖ Click on the File menu at the left edge of the ribbon at the top of the Query Editor.

❖ On the menu generated, click the Save Option. This will generate a dialog box with three buttons

   o Apply

   o Apply Later

   o Cancel.

At this point, you have to decide whether or not the changes you made in the Query Editor should be applied to the original data file imported into the Power BI Desktop. Selecting the Apply option will do just that, it will apply the changes made in the Query Editor to the original data file.

The Apply later option will save the changes made to the data file in the Query Editor, but it won't change the original file in the Power BI Desktop. Doing this only saves the changes made to the data file in Query Editor, leaving the original data file in its untouched state.

The Cancel option cancels the Save action you just carried out. Choose the option that serves your purpose best.

How to Exit the Query Editor

You already learned how to exit the Query Editor in Chapter 3, but that was just the basic way of exiting the Editor. There are more options that apply when leaving the Query Editor. To close the Query Editor carry out the following steps;

❖ Click the first button on the Home ribbon at the top of the Query Editor. This button is called the Close & Apply button. It will immediately update the original data file with all the transformations that took place in the Query Editor and exit to the Power BI Desktop window.

❖ If you want to have other options, click on the small triangle below the Close & Apply button. This will generate a pop-up menu with two options.

    o Apply

    o Close

The Apply option will perform the same activities as the Close & Apply button.

The Close option will close the Query Editor without applying the changes made in the editor to the original data file. It is best to save the transformation made in the Query Editor before choosing the option to prevent loss of data. When you click the Close option, a small notification box will be generated at the top of the Power BI

Desktop data window, imploring you to apply the changes made in the Query Editor.

The Query Editor is a very powerful tool for editing in the Power BI Desktop, not all users know how to handle and perform operations with the tool. But for those skilled in using the tool, and for you reading this book (this chapter to be precise), cleaning, filtering, modifying, and transforming your raw data file won't be so difficult. Once you know how to edit your data in the Query Editor, any problems that may occur during the creation of reports will not be from incorrect or improperly structured data. Not all the buttons or features were explained in this chapter, just the basic and popular editing steps carried out with the Query Editor were explained. With practice, you will be able to perform any transformation you want with the tool.

Chapter Five

Data Models

How to Create a Data Model in Power BI

In Power BI, creating a great visualization is essential, and to achieve this, you will need an excellent source of data for that. To be precise, there is a need for specific and correct data to be inputted into the data model of the Power BI, this way, millions of data from multiple sources can be utilized to build a framework on which you can base your dashboards and analyses. Once your data is accessible, there is still a need for a few ground works to be carried out. As you learned earlier, using query to search, input, and edit your raw data is basic in the preparation of data for a Data model.

This chapter is going to cover how to create data, model data, and convert inputted data into a well-structured dataset. This well-structured Dataset makes it easy for you to analyze your data, get perception and information from the inputted Dataset. The few topics to be covered are

> ➢ Defining data types

> ➢ Exploiting Tables

> ➢ Creating hierarchies

> ➢ Creating a joining or relationship between tables

- Classifying data

- Arranging data in the data model

- Creating a sort-by column that secures the dashboard element in the right sort order

Establishing the relationships between tables is the most basic aspect of data modeling. You must ensure that your Power BI desktop can derive the relationship between data on one table and another to get an accurate and precise result.

N.B- Data modeling can only be done when the data has been inputted into the Power BI desktop model, i.e., any data changes that occur in the Query editor must be applied before returning to the Power Desktop BI to prevent inaccurate results.

Power BI's Data View Window

When you import data into your BI Desktop, the default Data View ribbons- Home and Modelling will come into view. The second ribbon, Modeling, is used for organizing and classifying data and tables. It is also used to add calculated metrics and column. The Modeling ribbon contains a series of buttons, and their functions are shown in the table below:

Button	Function
New measure	It allows the addition of a new calculation to a table (Data).
Home Table	This button allows you to pick a table that will contain your calculations or value.
New table	It allows you to create a new table in the data file.

Data type	The button helps to outline the type of data you want in a particular column.
New column	This button is in control of the addition of a newly calculated column to a table.
Sort by column	This button helps you select the column containing data that can be used for sorting the data in another column.
Manage relationships	This button allows you to merge tables (this merging are referred to as relationships) and also delete them.
Format	This helps you define the way numbers will be formatted in a table.

Before you start creating your own data model, it is important to get familiar with the tools that will make the process easy to navigate after running the Power BI Desktop. To achieve this;

- Import all the queries to be used.

- Switch to the Data View where all tables are visible by clicking on the Data view icon on the left side of the window.

The Data View window is very similar to the Query Editor window, but there are some major differences between them. One of them is that only a sample of your data can be seen in Query Editor while all the dataset are made available in Data View once it has been imported into the data model. Another difference between them is that in Data view, you are working with the entire dataset and modifications are made in line with the dashboard requirement and specification. A major similarity is that they can both be used to create calculated columns.

N.B- Always remember that Query Editor is for searching, clarifying, and merging up while Data View is for enhancing and computing metrics in your data model. Also, note that you have to close your Query Editor before modeling your data.

Defining Data Types

There are nine different data types available to you on the Power BI desktop. When you transfer files from an external source, the Power BI desktop will try to change it to fit one of the nine data types. The nine different data are listed below with their description:

Data type	Description
Decimal numbers	Data types in this category are saved as real numbers, and they have a maximum 15 significant decimal numbers.
Fixed decimal numbers	This saves data as numbers, with the number of decimal specified.
Whole numbers	The data are saved as positive or negative integers, i.e., 2^63 and -2^63
Date and Time	Data are saved in the form of date and time on the Power BI Desktop. The dates are valid from January 1st, 1900.
Date	Saves data in the form of date
Time	Saves data in the form of time

Text	Data are saved in the form of 536,870,912 bytes of a Unicode string.
True / False	The data are saved in a True or False format (Boolean).
Binary	Data are saved in the form of 0 and 1.

NB: When using fixed decimal numbers, it is easier to avoid the overflow of calculation errors that occur when using an ordinary decimal number. Also using decimal numbers creates additional storage.

Exploiting Tables

After you have successfully imported and transformed your data, your next plan should be to exploit and manipulate the tables. Tables will be used in place of data because it is mostly the result generated when data are transformed in the Query Editor. Manipulating tables involves the following:

➢ *How to rename a table*

➢ *How to delete a table*

➢ *How to rename a column*

➢ *How to delete a column*

➢ *Setting width to a column*

How to Rename a Table

Imagine you don't feel comfortable with the name of a particular table that has successfully been transformed and imported from the Query Editor, and you wish to change or modify it to another, there are a series of steps to be taken to achieve this;

* ❖ Go to the field list which is on the right side of the Power BI Desktop window, there you will see the name of the table listed.

* ❖ Right-click on the name, this will generate a menu.

* ❖ On the menu, click on rename.

* ❖ Input the new name or modify the former name

* ❖ Press enter

Remember that Table is the result generated from the transformation of data by the query, so changing the name of a table will also change the name of the query

How to Delete a Table

This process is similar to that of changing the name of a table, but instead of clicking on rename, you click delete. This action will remove the table, including the series of query that has been used in transforming it. Due to this, the Power BI Desktop will ask for confirmation before carrying out this task because any mistake can make you lose not only your table but also your transformation steps.

Now that you are well acquainted with how to manipulate a table, you need to be able to perform similar actions within the table.

How to Rename a Column in the Power BI Desktop

Changing the name of a column is a simple and direct action that involves a couple of steps, which is pretty similar to renaming a table, with the only difference being the selection of a column instead of a table. You cannot use a name that is already existing for another column.

When renaming your column, you should put into considerations the Power BI questions and answer natural language features which will recognize a name that is mostly used in queries. Also renaming a particular column that is in a different visualization can cause confusion for you, so it is better to give this column a name you are comfortable that will cut across the dashboard. This allows the same data to have the same name.

How to Delete a Column in the Power BI Desktop

This is also similar to the process of deleting a table that was discussed earlier, deleting a column has some advantages in that it helps reduces the memory needed to store a dataset. It also helps to increase the time of refresh operations. This action also has a permanent effect that cannot be recovered by the undo and refreshing actions. Deleting a column by mistake can be recovered by shutting the file without saving it. Reopening the file will make it revert the previous version containing the deleted column. Another method is adding the name of the deleted column back in the source query.

Setting Width to a Column

Setting the column width is very crucial because this gives certain readability to your data, i.e., it makes it much easier to understand your data. It is quite simple and straightforward to achieve this, you can do so with the following steps;

- ❖ Place your cursor on the column you wish to adjust the width

- ❖ The cursor is placed in the column title over its right-hand limit

- ❖ Adjust the cursor to the left or right depending on your choice

Creating Hierarchies

Creating hierarchies is important in the organization of data, it helps you to create a structure for your work. This structure helps to understand better the information you are trying to get across. When creating hierarchies, the following steps are to be taken;

- ❖ Switch your Power BI desktop to report view

- ❖ Click on the stock table

- ❖ This will take you to a field, right-click on it. In the new hierarchy, this will be the top-level element.

- ❖ Click on new hierarchy (make hierarchy will appear which consists of Make field serving as the top-level element).

- ❖ The model Field is then dragged to the newly created hierarchy title.

Then you are done creating your hierarchy. This can then be used to create a table by dragging it to the report canvas where multiple elements that make up the canvas is put into use. This gives you access to the data in any visual. They also make starting material for drill-down charts and matrices. Renaming and deleting of any level in the hierarchy or the hierarchy itself is also possible if you are not comfortable with it.

Creating Joining's between Tables

Creating a joining (also referred to as relationship) between tables is fundamental when you want to create a logical and useable dataset. A Table relationship occurs when links exist between tables containing data. This allows the column of data in one table to be used in another table. A typical example is Invoices line and Invoice tables. They have been created in such a way that meaningless data duplication can be avoided. The technique used to create this table is referred to as relational modeling. Both invoice line and invoice table share a field that links them together in a way that allows the user to see data from both tables. Any element in both tables that would have repeated is seen in the header table i.e. invoice table, while the non-repeating data are stored in a detailed table, i.e., Invoice line table. Although it is possible to store this data in one table, it will create unnecessary repetitions that will increase the size of the Power BI files. Real-world data that are imported from other database have such links existing between them. When you decide to use multiple data source for your analysis, create a link that joins the table in a common field. If you are knowledgeable about SQL, it is easier to create a relationship between the tables from the source using the Query Editor. This helps to reduce the creation of unnecessary new tables.

Relationship View

Relationship view allows you to view your entire dataset as a whole without bordering you with the details. It gives an overview of your entire data tables, Also you can view those tables that are already joined together. Power BI tries to derive any possible relationship existing between the relationships yourself. You can view your data in the relationship view by simply clicking on the relationship view button at the left of the Power BI desktop. The relationship view also helps in maximizing and minimizing tables. This can be carried out by clicking the maximizing or minimizing button at the right of the table name tables and creates this relationship automatically. It saves you time and effort.

How to Create Relationships

Knowing the fields linking two or more tables is very important because it makes it easier to establish a relationship between them. You should also take note that on Power BI desktop, tables can only be joined together if they are in a single field.

How to Create Relationships Manually

You can also identify the tables and field you want to use to establish a relationship. It is not necessary to be in a relationship view before you create a relationship between these tables. Creating a relationship can also be carried out manually through the following steps;

❖ Pick a table that you wish to appear in the relationship.

❖ On the Home ribbon, click on the Manage Relationship button. This will generate a Manage Relationship dialog box.

❖ On the manage relationship dialog, choose "new." This will take you to the Create Relationship dialog box.

❖ Click on invoice table from the list of tables that pops up in the upper part of the dialog.

❖ Choose an invoice line table at the lower part of the dialog. An invoice-ID field that will establish a relationship will appear automatically. Also, if the Power BI already derived the field, it will establish the relationship, if not or if it chooses the wrong field, you can pick the correct field. Then click okay, this should return you to the manage relationship dialog.

❖ When you are done creating the dialog, close the manage relationship dialog. The relationship will be established.

How to Create a Relationship Automatically

Like it was mentioned earlier in the chapter, Power BI can automatically guess whether a relationship exists between two tables. You can set the Power BI desktop to be able to detect these relationships when you are working. This has a major advantage because it helps reduce the manual work that goes into creating these relationships yourself, also it greatly reduces the risk of an error occurring between tables. However, this is relative. To carry out this process is very simple and straightforward, follow the steps below;

❖ On the Home ribbon, click on the Manage Relationship button. A Manage Relationship dialog box will pop up.

❖ On the manage relationship dialog, select AutoDetect, this will bring out the detected relationships found by Power BI desktop.

❖ Click close to activate the selection. All relationships, both pre-established relationship and those created through Auto detection will be listed in the relationship management dialog.

❖ You can now return to the relationship view by selecting close.

How to Delete a Relationship

There are times when you will need to remove a relationship that you no longer want or a relationship created by mistake. To perform this task, you simply need to;

❖ Go to the Home ribbon, select the design view. This will display all the tables in the relationship view.

❖ Click on the relationship to be deleted, this will highlight the two tables and the arrow connecting them becomes a double link.

❖ You can press delete from your keyboard or right click your mouse, and select delete, Power BI desktop will bring out a confirmation dialog, select delete. And you're done.

Managing Relationships

Learning how to manage relationships is crucial, especially if you want to alter a field that serves as the foundation of a relationship. This is also useful when you are trying to create or delete several relationships at the same time. The process of creating and deleting several relationships is similar to those discussed earlier. Managing a relationship can be described as the key to creating effective and operative data model. To manage a relationship, you have to:

❖ Click on the Manage Relationship button on the home ribbon. A manage relationship dialog box will appear.

❖ Select the relationship you want to modify

❖ Double click on the relationship and select edit, this will bring out the edit dialog

❖ Modify the relationship.

You also have the option of deactivating relationships. This occurs when you no longer want a relationship to exist between two tables, and you don't want to delete it. Go to the manage relationship dialog, unselect the table in the active box. The same process applies for reactivating a relationship. However, the edit relationship dialog has an advanced option that might be useful on some occasions, they are Cardinality and cross filter direction. Cardinality helps you to outline the number of column in a table that is associated with a similar column in the joined table. Cross filter directions define whether a filter can be used for all the tables in a related group of tables or in one particular table where the aggregation is carried out.

NB: If a set of joined tables are deleted, reimporting the tables will not bring back the created relationship unless the joining are also reimported, i.e., once a set of Joined table is deleted, Power BI Desktop will not remember the relationship between them, such that any relationship that exists between them has to be created manually.

Classifying Data

The dashboard is made up of hyperlinks, facts, figure, and geographical data. A human can invariably recognize hyperlinks, but that is not always the case for the Power BI. So to make your work easier, you have to classify the column that house these types of data. For example, if you want a table that will contain cities as the data source;

❖   Choose a city table in the field list

❖   Select the column containing the city name (this will be highlighted).

❖   Select the box to the right of the data category button, a context menu will appear

❖   Select a city from the menu

There are different data category options to pick from when classifying data. Few of these categories are listed below:

➢   Uncategorized: This encompasses all data that are not involved in the creation of mapping or hyperlinks.

➢   City: Indicates a city for creating maps

➢   Web URL: Specifies a URL used for hyperlinks

➢   Barcodes: This shows the fields containing the barcodes

There are also several other data category options apart from the once above, such as country, continent, place, latitude, postal code, image URL, state, province, longitude, etc. They are all used for creating mappings.

Even though you do not specify the data, the Power BI can still create maps in the Dashboard, the downside of this is that the result will have a slim chance of being a success. Nevertheless, if you specify that a column holds a particular type of data, this can be avoided.

Arranging Data in the Data Model

When you create an arrangement for the data in a table, Power BI allows the arrangement to be used in all the visualizations across the dashboard. Creating an arrangement reduces the problem of creating several repetitive operations, and it saves time. This is achieved by creating a format, which will be applicable across all visualizations. The data are better understood when there is a format defining it.

How to Format a Column

❖ Select from the field list the name of the table containing the column you wish to arrange

❖ Click the inside of the column that you want to format

❖ Select the thousand-separator icon from the modeling ribbon. The appearance of all the figure in this column will change to a thousand separator and two decimals.

If you don't want a format for your figure and you wish to return it to the plain data, you can click on the general format. Also note that unlike excel, you can only format a whole column and not just a range of figures. The selection of several adjacent columns and formatting it in a single operation is not possible for Power BI desktop. The general principle operated by the Format once and then application of your formatting. When formatting, you should note that Date and time Format cannot be applied if the data does not contain date and time. In other words, the column containing data can only be formatted with the format option that applies to it.

There are several format options available for use:

Format option	Description
General	The data are left unformatted
Currency	It creates two decimal places and a thousand separator between figures. It also gives your figure a monetary symbol

Date and time	It gives date and time format
Whole number	It gives your figure a thousand separator and then removes any decimal point
Percentage	The percentage symbol is added as a prefix. It also multiplies your figure by 100.
Scientific text	Gives your figure a scientific arrangement
Boolean	Your figures are presented in the true/false format
Binary	Your data are represented in the 0 and 1 format
Decimal number	Gives your figure a thousand separator that has two decimals

The Power BI desktop also has a wide range of currency format to choose from if the data you are dealing with involves currency. You just need to select the one you will be working with. The series of steps below show you how to do that;

- At the right of the currency icon, there is a downward-facing triangle, click on it, it will bring out a variety of format.

- Choose your currency symbol of choice.

Creating Sort- By for Data Model

If you want to search for a dataset in a visualization that is based on the content of another column, you have to use the sort-by column. For example, if you have a data table containing month sales. If you sort this by month name, it will give you an alphabetical arrangement of the month rather than starting with January, your column will start from April. To avoid this, you can sort this data based on the month number with January being the first.

❖ Load your sample file

❖ Go to data view, from the field list, choose the date dimension, this will bring out the date data

❖ Highlight the column by selecting the of the month full column

❖ Select the sort-by column from the modeling ribbon, this will display the list of column available

❖ Select month number

This way your month name has been sorted by the factor of their month number, this will display the month name from January and not in alphabetical order. You can also remove the sort-by column from a data if it is not needed by selecting the sort-by column button and then picking the original column name.

How to Hide Fields and Tables from Users

There may be some excess columns in your data that may not be useful in the creation of your report. The columns may be there because;

• The column already exists in hierarchies.

- The column contains data that are not needed yet but will serve future purposes

- The column will be used for intermediate calculation

- Sort-by column

At a point, the columns might be too much and clutter your work. When this happens, you will need to hide some of the columns that are not relevant to your analysis. This helps in the clarification of your work should a new user want to use the data created by you, because it will eliminate the confusion of seeing so many columns and guarantee that only the important data are available.

When you want to hide a table or file, all you need to do is

❖ Select the table you want to conceal

❖ On the popup menu, go to report view and click hide

Once you are done with the process, the table will be hidden from view, and this achieves your goal of reducing the clutter in your work. You are now left with essential data needed for your analysis.

Using a Calculated Column to Extend Data Models

Power BI Desktop makes most of the calculations easy to carry out. The first thing you need to know is that in the Power BI desktop, not all data models need extensive calculation. Some data are self-explanatory without the need to brush it up, but at a point, there will be a need for you to apply basic mathematics to work like calculation of percentage or even comparing figures.

DAX, which is an acronym for Data Analysis eXpression, is the language written for calculations in power desktop BI. It is a formula language program because it is made up of over 300 formulas that can be used alone or combine to create metrics. This formula is almost similar to those found in Excel.

Types of Calculation

When your imported data contains all that is needed to create your visualization, Power BI will make your life much easier. But this is not always the case, there is still a metric to be calculated or added to tables leading to the extension of data. A tool like Power BI desktop requires just the addition of all metrics both calculated and imported from the source to the dataset and not the output. The probability of an error being in your work is reduced. Components that will be of important use to your dashboard are also created when creating DAX metrics, the components include;

> ➢ Addition of components used in filtering visualizations

> ➢ Creation of component used in the classification of data, e.g., grouping

> ➢ Creation of derived metrics that will be seen in the visualization

> ➢ Creation of new metrics that are based on the existing metrics

> ➢ Adding specific calculations of your own

> ➢ Creating order and rank for your Data

> ➢ Addition of weightings to value

> ➢ Addition of the new column to a dataset

Creating and adding a new column to a dataset is one of the two ways a dataset can be extended. Reasons why you might want to extend your current dataset:

- Connecting the data from two already existing column to give a new column

- When carrying out fundamental calculations such as addition and subtraction in every row of a table for more than one column

- When you extract the part of a data in one column to another column where you need it

- When you extract from the date column, the date element to a new column

- When you want to extract a part of data from a column to a new column

There are still several other reasons for extending a dataset, but the important thing is that at a point, the need will arise to extend a current dataset. There are several ways of extending a dataset, and these ways are very similar to that of Excel. The knowledge of extending dataset is based on that of Excel, i.e., the function, extension techniques, and the way it is designed all follow the same pattern as excel. You should also note that when a formula whether derived or existing in the Power BI, is added from the start to a column, and a new column is created, this formula also applies to the new column. The data can only be recalculated when you refresh your source data.

Connecting Column Contents

Sometimes when you import data from a different source, you can have two columns containing the data you need. The best thing is to merge the columns and connect them. To achieve this, you have to be able to concatenate the data into one column. For example, you want to create a column containing the make and model for flashy cars, and this data are imported from a different source. You need to create a new column that will take the data from both columns. The steps below explain how to join the columns together:

- ❖ Open the data file in Power desktop BI and activate the data view

- ❖ Open the Stock table by clicking on it.

- ❖ Go to the modeling ribbon and select New Column. The new column will appear on the right side of the final column.

- ❖ The text displayed in the formula box will look like this *Column=*

- ❖ After the Equals sign in the formula bar, press the "[" symbol on your keyboard. This will display all the fields in the table.

- ❖ In the pop-up list of columns, double click a field, go to the formula box and add & " " &, the formula box will display [Name of the field you selected] & " "&.

- ❖ Repeat the actions above and click on another field in the list generated, the formula box will display [Name of the first field] & " "& [Name of the second field]

- ❖ When you are done, press Enter to activate the instructions. The two fields selected will be joined together.

- ❖ Click the column header and type in a new name for your column.

NB:

As it was said earlier, this process is very similar to that of Excel, so for a user familiar with Excel, this would be a walkover. Despite the similarities to Excel, some differences that exist between them, for instance;

- Any newly created column is always on the right side of an existing column and cannot be shifted elsewhere.

- Also, when you are creating a function, it must start with the equality sign.

- Another difference is that the column is referenced rather than a cell, unlike Excel where the cell can be referenced.

- The names of columns are always inside square brackets.

In the field list, new columns are always designated with a small Fx icon so they can be distinguished from other fields.

How to Modify Text

DAX offers you a variety of functions that can help in the modification and standardization of a text. For example, if you have a data file containing information on the names and address of your clients and you want to modify the text in such a way that the new column will contain acronyms of the names of the clients. To achieve this, you have to carry out the following process;

- ❖ Open the data file in Power desktop BI and activate the data view

- ❖ Open the Stock table by clicking on it.

❖ Go to the modeling ribbon and select New Column. The new column will appear on the right side of the final column.

❖ The text displayed in the formula box will look like this *Column=*

❖ Type LEFT after the equality symbol

❖ Click your preferred function once it appears in the popup menu, click the inside of the column containing your text, then press comma.

❖ Since the acronym is going to be three characters, enter or press 3, this will tell the left function that you are isolating the first three characters for each row, click or press)

❖ Rename the column as Name Abbreviation and press enter.

The Power BI desktop contains some core text functions: LEFT (), RIGHT (), MID (), UPPER (), LOWER (). The first two extract a specific number of characters from the left and right column, while the mid extract a specified number of character from specific positions inside the column. The last two do not require any parameter but are used in the conversion of data to either upper case or lower case.

How to Carry out Simple Calculations

It has been established that carrying out basic calculations is one of the ways by which original data can be extended. Sometimes while doing our data analysis, there is a need to carry out simple calculations. Calculations are also needed when we are comparing figures, e.g., if you want to know the percentage of cars your company sold between the last month and the present one. In Power BI Desktop, some core math operators are used to carry out our calculations. You are probably familiar with the math operators listed below:

➢ Addition operators (+)

➢ Subtraction operators (-)

➢ Division operators (/)

➢ Multiplication operators (*)

Once again, this will be familiar to the Excel users. The arithmetic calculation in Power BI desktop is the same as that of Excel and much easier because you don't have to apply the formula individually to the row, it automatically applies to all the rows. There are still a few differences, like the appearance of a table on the right rather than at the bottom in excel. There is no formula button present like it is in excel. You should note when carrying out all these operations, your Power Desktop BI must be in data view, for example, you want to know the direct cost involved in the purchase of a fridge, this includes the purchase cost and all other cost incurred whether during transportation.

❖ Click the stock table

❖ On the modeling ribbon, Click New Column

❖ Name the Column

❖ Go to the list of fields and enter the name of the column you want to reference and select it.

❖ In this order type

— minus sign

— left square bracket

❖   Choose the transportation column and enter the right square column, you are going to have something like this on your screen

❖   cost = [cost price] – [transportation price]

❖   Press enter, a new column containing your solved data will be created

At this stage, you are already modifying your data's successfully, another modification to your data is rounding values, you can either round up or round down your figures to the nearest value. Power BI contains several functions for carrying out this task.

Selecting the Right Table for Joined Calculations

In Power BI Desktop, data can only be imported to a column if the column you are importing from is made up of reference data or sub value of the current column. You cannot import data from columns that are made up of reference data, e.g., a table containing countries, color, etc. But data can be imported from tables like invoice table because they contain original data. Power BI can be used to perform other operations apart from carrying basic calculations, such operations include safe division, counting reference elements, carrying out the statistical function, creating a specific format for calculation, etc.

How to carry out Logical Functions

Logical functions include IF, NESTED IF, and others, we are moving on from the easy use of Power BI to a more complex use. The exception indicator is very important, and they help in comparing facts and figures. Now let's go into how you can use the exception indicator IF in your data analysis.

- ❖   Create a new column, at the right of the equal symbol, press IF

- ❖   Enter the right bracket [

- ❖   Select the column you want to use for comparison in the list and enter any of the comparison operators

- ❖   Enter the value you are using for your comparison, put a comma after this

- ❖   Enter your text (make sure the text is in double-quotes) and add the closing parenthesis, it should look like this

- ❖   = IF ([your selected column] > value, "your text")

- ❖   Press enter, this will perform the operation such that any row that is greater than your value will display your text

- ❖   You can now rename the column.

The greater than (>) symbol is part of the comparison operators used in Power BI desktop, other comparison operators include

— Equality (=)

— Not equal to (<>)

— Less than (>)

— Greater than or equal to (>=)

— Less than or equal to (<=)

The IF function can carry out about three arguments. When the content of the column is compared to a fixed value, the outcome, the test is true. The first two arguments are compulsory for the IF function, while the third argument is optional, and this is the outcome of if it is false. Most times, the focus is always on the first two arguments.

How to carry out the Nested IF Function

Often time in data analysis, there is a need to classify your data by a range of values. To achieve this, you need the nested IF, i.e. one IF inside another IF. The test will be applied to all the three possible outcomes as compared to the IF function in which the third argument is optional. For example, if you want to separate cars in a column into low, medium and high mileage, the steps are very similar to that of the IF function

❖ Create a new column and to the left of the equal sign, enter Class and to the right enter IF

❖ Enter the square bracket, this will give you the field list

❖ Select mileage and enter <= 10000 (remember this is your comparison value), press comma

❖ Type "low," it must be in double quotes, press comma

❖ Press IF and open a bracket

❖ Select mileage and enter <= 15000, press the comma

❖ Enter the "medium, "high," these two must always be in double-quotes, and a comma must be in between the two

❖ Press two right bracket, one for each IF function

❖ Click enter

When performing a task in nested IF, it must follow a logical sequence such that the Nested IF is acting as a hoop. This way, you get appropriate results for your tests. When categorizing data, it can sometimes involve the use of logic where two or more conditions applied to the evaluation of data. When using the logic function, you can test more columns for a condition. The logic function is limited to the application of two parameters, i.e., only two logic operators can be applied at the same time. The logical operators are the AND (&&), OR (||) and NOT (|).

How to Add Measures to a Data Model

Adding a new column to data always leads to the addition of extra data to your data model, but the addition of metrics to a data can perform all the analysis needed for your work, especially when your formula application is for the whole table and not rows in a column. In general, you need another formula for that can apply to your table as a whole. This type of formula is referred to as a simple measure or metrics. This simple metrics can give a powerful result that can be of great help to your analysis. This simple measure can perform analysis that cannot be done in a calculated column.

To carry out a simple measure;

- ❖   Load your Power BI data file

- ❖   Go to the data view

- ❖   Choose the table to wish you are adding the measure

- ❖   Select the new measure button in the modeling ribbon

- ❖   Add your formula to the formula box

- ❖   Select the table, to wish the measure will derive analysis

- ❖   Press enter to confirm your creation.

NB: Unlike the addition of new column in the dataset, there is no new column created for your data in measures, the only proof that it exists is when the table is expanded, it can be seen in the field list. Measures in the field list can be renamed by right-clicking the measure name and selecting Rename from the pop-up list. One important thing to observe is that a properly applied measure can be used in any visualization, table, and chart. When applied to this, it will give the correct result. Measures can also be applied to hierarchies of data. When measures applied to a visualization gives calculations that are in decimal places, but you don't need the data in decimals, apply format measures. This process is the same with format column in Power Desktop BI.

Carrying Out Basic Aggregations

When learning measures, you will become acquainted with the DAX functions because they are DAX formulae. Many of the techniques that were discussed earlier in the creation of column can be applied when creating your measures. Like it was mentioned earlier, to perform these operations, your Power Desktop BI must be in the data view.

❖ Click the stock table

❖ On the modeling ribbon, select New Measure

❖ Name the measure

❖ To the right of the equal sign, enter the function Sum, then press the left parenthesis.

❖ Enter the left bracket to restrict the field list in the current table

❖ Type your field name, this will display all tables with the field name

❖   Select the field you want for the operation

❖   Press the right parenthesis then click enter. This should display your formula, You can now arrange this column to suit what you want

Note that if there are several fields with the same name as that of the field you are using, you add the table name to your field name so data the power desktop BI, is sure that it is using the correct field from the correct table. Table's names should be in single quotes if it contains spaces and field name must be confined in a square bracket.

Measures can also be created by combining several DAX functions. These measures are known as multiple measures. For example, you want to apply a ratio calculation to a table, it is similar to the steps for basic aggregation of measures above but in step 8 above, paste or type your formula and then press enter. Measures can also be applied across all field in a data model.

Data filtering in measures

Sometimes using the filter in the Power BI desktop does not give us the expected results. Some of the reasons for this can be that we want a specific filter for a single metric or you are developing a complex formula created for a specific purpose. This might require you to filter your data in measures. There are different types of filter

➢ *Simple filters* – This tool allows you to apply a series of filter to a measure that you can apply when creating a visual on your dashboard. It helps you to concentrate on a selected subset of data. Example of simple filters are

    o   Text filters

- o   Numeric filters

➢   *Complex filters* – In the real world of data analysis, filtering of data is not always so simple. For example, when you want to apply multiple filters to data, calculating the percentage of totals, ALL EXCEPT function.

Another thing you need to understand is the filter context, which creates the basis for a dynamic data analysis. There are three key elements of the filter context. They include

➢   Row context

➢   Query context

➢   Filter context

Data measure is a broad subject. A measure can be used to carry out a lot of functions. As you familiarize yourself with the use of DAX, there are few tips that will help you along the way. The first tip is to use a calculated column, they make your work much easier and do not take up space. That means more space will be available on your disk and in the memory. By default, all calculated columns and measures are recalculated by Power BI desktop when there is a change in data set. The main reasons why recalculation occurs are

- When external source data has been filtered.

- When you rename a table or column.

- When you a new calculation to an existing measure or column.

- When an external source of data has been updated.

Conclusion

With what you have read in the chapters of the book, you can see that it really is a comprehensive beginner guide for learning the basics of Power BI. What is in this book can help you create data models, reports, and visualizations for your business or organization. If you read the tutorials and instructions given in the book thoroughly, you will have an idea of how to operate and use every feature Power BI boasts of. However, if you want to dig deeper into what Power BI has to offer, you will need an advanced guide that will take you farther into the Business Intelligence tool. Advanced guide books will cover more about the DAX language and how to use it to create and edit data models on Power BI.

Resources

www.techtarget.com

Adam Aspin (2018), *Pro Power BI Desktop*: Interactive data analysis and visualization for the desktop. Apress

Johansen A. (2016), *Python: The Ultimate Beginner's Guide!* CreateSpace Independent Publishing Platform.

Alberto Ferrari and Marco Russo (2016), *Introducing Microsoft Power BI*. Microsoft Press.

Alberto Ferrari and Marco Russo (2017), *Analyzing Data with Microsoft Power BI and Power Pivot for Excel*. Microsoft Press.

Brett Powell (2018), Mastering Microsoft Power BI. Microsoft Press.

Dan Clark (2016), *Beginning Power BI with Excel 2013: Self-Service Business Intelligence Using Power Pivot, Power View, Power Query, and Power Map*. Apress.

Made in the USA
Middletown, DE
27 February 2020